Indian Missions

A Critical Bibliography

By JAMES P. RONDA
and JAMES AXTELL

D1065918

The Newberry Library Center for the History
of the American Indian Bibliographical Series
Francis Jennings, General Editor

UNIVERSITY LIBRARY
UW-STEVENS POINT

Indian Missions

BIBLIOGRAPHICAL SERIES
The Newberry Library Center
for the History of the American Indian

General Editor
Francis Jennings

The Center Is Supported by Grants from

The National Endowment for the Humanities
The Ford Foundation
The W. Clement and Jessie V. Stone Foundation
The Woods Charitable Fund, Inc.

Indian Missions

A Critical Bibliography

JAMES P. RONDA
and
JAMES AXTELL

Published for the Newberry Library

Indiana University Press

BLOOMINGTON AND LONDON

Copyright © 1978 by Indiana University Press
All rights reserved

No part of this book may be reproduced or utilized in any form or by any means, electronic or mechanical, including photocopying and recording, or by any information storage and retrieval system, without permission in writing from the publisher. The Association of American University Presses' Resolution on Permissions constitutes the only exception to this prohibition.

Manufactured in the United States of America

Library of Congress Cataloging in Publication Data
Ronda, James P 1943-
Indian missions.
(Bibliographical series - The Newberry Library, Center for the History of the American Indian)
Includes index.
1. Indians of North America--Missions--Bibliography.
I. Axtell, James L., joint author. II. Title.
III. Series: Bibliographical series.
Z1209.2.N67R65   [E98.M6]   016.266'00973   78-3253
ISBN 0-253-32978-7   1 2 3 4 5 82 81 80 79 78

Z
1209.2
.N67
R65

CONTENTS

309553

THE EDITOR TO THE READER

A massive literature exists for the history and culture of American Indians, but the quality of that literature is very uneven. At its best it compares well with the finest scholarship and most interesting reading to be found anywhere. At its worst it may take the form of malicious fabrication. Sometimes well-intentioned writers give false impressions of reality either because of their own limitations of mind or because they lack adequate information. The consequence is a kind of chaos through which advanced scholars as well as new students must warily pick their way. It is, after all, a history of hundreds, if not thousands, of human communities spread over an entire continent and enduring through millennia of pre-Columbian years as well as the five centuries that Europeans have documented since 1492. That is not a small amount of history.

Often, however, historians have been so concerned with the affairs of European colonies or the United States that they have almost omitted Indians from their own history. There is a way of writing "frontier history" and the "history of Indian-White relations" that often focuses so narrowly upon the intentions and desires of Euro-Americans as to treat Native Americans as though they were merely natural parts of the landscape, like forests or mountains or wild animals — obstacles to "progress" or "civilization." One of the major purposes of the Newberry Library's Center for the History of the American

Indian is to modify that narrow conception; to put Indians properly back into the central role in their own history and into the history of the United States of America as well — as participants in, rather than obstacles to, the creation of American society and culture.

The series of bibliographies of which this book is one part is intended as a guide to reliable sources and studies in particular fields of the general literature. Some of these are devoted to culture areas; others treat selected individual tribes; and a third group speaks to significant contemporary and historical issues.

This work is designed in a format, standard for the series, intended to be useful to both beginning students and advanced scholars. It has two main parts: the essay (conveniently organized by subheadings) and an alphabetical list of all works cited. All citations in the essay are directly keyed, by means of bracketed numbers, to the more complete publication data in the list; and each item in the list carries a cross-reference to the page number where it is mentioned in the essay. In addition, the series incorporates several information-at-a-glance features. Among them are two sets of recommended titles: a list of five works recommended for the beginner and a group of volumes that constitute a basic library collection in the field. The large, complete list also uses asterisks to denote works suitable for secondary school students. This apparatus has been built in because the bibliographical essay, in a form familiar to scholars, could prove fairly hard going for beginners, who may wish to put it aside until they have gained sufficient background from introductory materials. Such students should come back to the essay eventually, however, because it surveys a vast sweep of information about a great variety of persons, places, communities, and events.

There is variety also in the kinds of sources because these critical bibliographies support the study of ethno-history. Unlike older, more narrow disciplines, ethno-history embraces the entire culture of a people; it demands contributions from a wide range of source materials. Not the least of these in the history of American Indians are their own music, crafts, linguistics, and oral traditions. Whenever possible, the authors have included such sources as well as those associated with politics, economics, geography, and so on. It will be recognized that the variety of relevant sources will change with the nature of the topic discussed.

In the last analysis this work, like all other bibliographical devices, is a tool. Each author is an expert who knows the literature and advises what source is most helpful for which purpose, but students must use this help according to their individual purposes and capacities. Many ways suggest themselves. The decision is the reader's own.

RECOMMENDED WORKS

For the Beginner

[13]   Beaver, R. Pierce, *Church, State, and the American Indian.*

[16]   Berkhofer, Robert F., Jr., *Salvation and the Savage.*

[94]   Horgan, Paul, *Lamy of Sante Fe.*

[110]   Kellaway, William, *The New England Company.*

[192]   Wallace, Anthony F. C., *The Death and Rebirth of the Seneca.*

For a Basic Library Collection

[20]   Bowden, Henry Warner, "Spanish Missions, Cultural Conflict and the Pueblo Revolt of 1680."

[32]   Cook, Sherburne F., *The Conflict between the California Indian and White Civilization.*

[47]   Dunne, Peter Masten, *Pioneer Black Robes on the West Coast.*

[67]   Garraghan, Gilbert J., *The Jesuits of the Middle United States.*

[80]   Gray, Elma E., and Leslie Robb, *Wilderness Christians.*

BIBLIOGRAPHICAL ESSAY

Introduction

Throughout the long history of Indian-white relations, the Christian mission has played a crucial role. It has shaped events and changed lives as surely as any other human institution, often with far-reaching effects. In many ways its impact has been unique. As Europeans invaded the Indian domain, missionaries were nearly always in the vanguard, and their efforts influenced the behavior of both Indians and Europeans in many kinds of encounters. Within the Christian mission Native Americans and Europeans confronted each other in ways unknown in other arenas of culture contact. Missionaries alone required that Indians forsake their native religions and life-styles to adopt those of the invaders. Mission workers desired nothing less than a cultural revolution for the American Indian, and they hoped by their labors to bring it about. The history of Indian missions may rightly be interpreted as the story of that fascinating struggle.

Yet for centuries the historical image of the mission remained the same. Because the missionaries were usually dedicated and self-sacrificing in the pursuit of Indian souls, historians have revered them more than they

The authors would like to express their special thanks to Jeanne Ronda for her unstinting support, diligent research, and care for words.

have understood them. Because many missionaries were skilled propagandists, scholars have allowed their words — from mission reports, relations, letters, pamphlets, and autobiographies — to dominate our understanding of the mission. The classics of mission writing, such as *The Jesuit Relations*, the John Eliot tracts, Father Nicholas Point's words and pictures in *Wilderness Kingdom*, and *Life, Letters, and Travels of Father Pierre-Jean de Smet, S.J.*, all offer essentially the same interpretation of Indian mission history. Consumed with zeal, so runs the argument, missionaries struggled against nearly overwhelming odds to bring the joys of Christian salvation and the benefits of Western civilization to heathen savages. Those Native Americans who opposed the mission were dismissed as agents of the devil or, as in the case of Indian religious leaders, men jealous of their own personal influence. Such an ethnocentric perspective, with its harsh rhetoric of civilization-versus-savagery, pervaded Indian mission writing well into the present century. Whether one reads Stephen R. Riggs's autobiographical *Tah́-koo-wah-kań; or, The Gospel among the Dakotas* or Herbert Bolton's *Rim of Christendom: Biography of Eusebio Francisco Kino, Pacific Coast Pioneer*, the scenario is the same — valiant soldiers of the cross labor to do good and to overcome the forces of evil. The inspirational glow of such stories may blind us to the fact that they often deny the humanity and individual personality of both Indians and missionaries. Mission workers were always something more than evangelical soul-winners. They were potent agents for social change, dedicated to

the goal of transforming Indians into purified Europeans. At the same time, Indians were always more than
passive souls longing for spiritual and cultural salvation.
They were complex human beings capable of respond-
ing to the mission invasion in a variety of ways. Sadly,
most traditional accounts fail to acknowledge either their
complexity or this variety.

It has been only in the past two decades that history
has begun to replace hagiography in the study of Indian
missions. Using tools developed by anthropologists and
sociologists, historians are now beginning to look beyond
missionary rhetoric to examine the way missions actually
operated. At last they are viewing the mission as a crucial
arena for culture contact and change. The newer mission
studies are less interested in the number of mission buildings (and their architectural styles and construction
dates) than older accounts have been. They are much
more concerned with the cultural interaction that took
place within those walls. This approach offers a subtler
and more accurate historical understanding of both
Indian-white relations and Indian tribal history. It urges
us to acquire an awareness of Indian religions and to
apply insights from the history of missions outside North
America. Unlike most traditional studies, it offers attitudes and methods that can help to capture the cultural
and personal nuances of Indian mission activity.

The new Indian mission history has already yielded
two exciting insights. First, building upon the culture-
contact and acculturation studies of anthropologists in
the 1930s and 1940s, historians have discovered that the

missionary might be best viewed as a "cultural revolutionary," bent on the radical transformation of Indian
life. Anthropological fieldwork reports brought historians into the world of culture contact and gave them a
means to escape the tyranny of the "civilization-versus-
savagery" perspective. Recent books by Francis Paul
Prucha, *American Indian Policy in Crisis: Christian Reformers and the Indian, 1865–1900* [156], R. Pierce Beaver,
Church, State, and the American Indian [13], and George A.
Schultz, *An Indian Canaan: Isaac McCoy and the Vision of
an Indian State* [170] demonstrate in varying degrees an
understanding of the mission as a powerful force for
change. They illustrate the intimate relationship between programs promoted by missionaries and the secular designs of government bureaucrats intent on adding
more land to the growing American empire.

Second, historians have come to realize that Indian
responses to missionization deserve far more scholarly
attention. Taking their cue from African mission historians, these scholars have attempted to restore Indian
words and actions to their rightful place in the drama.
Traditional mission history simply ignored them. Most
scholars quickly dismissed Indian criticism of mission
tactics and missionary Christianity and hurried on to
narrate the growth of mission establishments as seen
through European eyes. Native American theologies
were considered unworthy of historical study. Missionaries were the principal actors, while Indians remained
the acted-upon, providing only the necessary souls for
salvation and bodies for Europeanization. The publica-

tion in 1965 of Robert F. Berkhofer's *Salvation and the Savage: An Analysis of Protestant Missions and American Indian Response, 1787–1862* [16] marked the beginning of what is now a major effort by many scholars to evaluate Indians as active participants in the mission situation. This significant direction in mission studies can be seen in a number of recent articles, including Henry Warner Bowden's "Spanish Missions, Cultural Conflict and the Pueblo Revolt of 1680" [20], George Harwood Phillips's "Indians and the Breakdown of the Spanish Mission System in California" [153], James P. Ronda's, " 'We Are Well as We Are': An Indian Critique of Early American Missions" [165], and Martha Voght's "Shamans and Padres: The Religion of the Southern California Mission Indians" [189].

Two examples typify the recent shift in perspectives. Missions in California and the Southwest have long had a special aura of romance. The "heroic" exploits of Jesuits and Franciscans dominate the work of Herbert Bolton and his students. That same conception of mission history has found expression in the writings of a Bolton student, Peter Masten Dunne. His *Pioneer Black Robes on the West Coast* [47] and *Black Robes in Lower California* [48] are narrative histories on a grand scale. They stand in sharp contrast to *The Conflict between the California Indian and White Civilization* by Sherburne F. Cook [32], who pioneered the use of demographic data for mission history. Cook relates a tale of Indian resistance and pragmatic accommodation to the rigors of mission life. To witness the same interpretive shift for missions in the

Southwest, one may compare Thomas Harwood's *History of New Mexico Spanish and English Missions of the Methodist Episcopal Church from 1850 to 1910* [85] or John Dolfin's *Bringing the Gospel in Hogan and Pueblo* [37] to recent studies that show cultures in collision. Robert N. Rapoport's "Changing Navajo Religious Values: A Study of Christian Missions to the Rimrock Navajos" [158] and Edward H. Spicer's impressive *Cycles of Conquest: The Impact of Spain, Mexico, and the United States on the Indians of the Southwest, 1533–1960* [177] offer the reader a fuller, multicultural vision of the mission in action. Even institutional studies have demonstrated this new awareness. Two books by John L. Kessell, *Mission of Sorrows: Jesuit Guevari and the Pimas, 1691–1767* [114] and *Friars, Soldiers, and Reformers: Hispanic Arizona and the Sonora Mission Frontier, 1767–1856* [115] display it. Clearly, the new scholarship on Southwest missions graphically illustrates the impact of ethnohistory on mission research.

Perhaps nowhere can the changing interpretations be better seen than in the traditional and revisionist accounts of missions in colonial New England. The tracts and pamphlets of John Eliot, [49-51], Eleazar Wheelock's *A Plain and Faithful Narrative . . . of the Indian Charity-School* [198], and Ola Elizabeth Winslow's laudatory *John Eliot "Apostle to the Indians"* [206] all feature the same interpretation. From the pages of these works, missionaries emerge as saints. Eliot, his co-workers, and his successors appear as men of unblemished virtue who defended Indians against land-hungry settlers and power-hungry colonial bureaucrats. In "Goals and Func-

tions of Puritan Missions to the Indians" [98], Francis
Jennings tells a very different story. Jennings's rigorous
study exposes the political role the Eliot mission played in
Massachusetts Bay's anti-Indian campaign. The political
dimension of Eliot's endeavors is also described in Neal
Salisbury's seminal essay "Red Puritans: The 'Praying
Indians' of Massachusetts Bay and John Eliot" [167]. In
this article, and in "Prospero in New England: The Puritan Missionary as Colonist" [168], Salisbury reveals the
ways the mission weakened and subverted tribal cultures
at a time of profound crisis. Taken together, these newer
studies offer a radically different story of Puritan missions and ably demonstrate the new approach to mission
history.

Denominational Variety

To speak of the Christian mission to Indians implies a
unity of purpose and organization that never existed. As
a consequence of the Protestant Reformation and the
forces of sectarianism released by that movement, the
missionary enterprise in North America was marked by
considerable denominational variety and competition.
The differences between Catholic missions and Protestant efforts are especially noteworthy, since they often
meant the difference between modest success and failure. Perhaps the best book to examine those differences
is Howard L. Harrod's superb *Mission among the Blackfeet*
[84]. Harrod's work compares Jesuit and Methodist
labors and describes the distinct approaches taken by the

"black robes" and the "short coats." The difference between priest and minister was striking. The Methodist missionary was locked into a ministerial role — a role that severely limited his ability to deal with the daily needs of both converts and traditionalists. He sought merely to build a congregation of converts, preach to that congregation, and expand its numbers. He saw no reason to tend to the secular needs of those outside his congregation. The Jesuit missionary found that his priestly role fit more naturally into Blackfoot life and allowed him to relate to Indians with greater ease and effectiveness. The priest, like his Indian counterpart, could care for the sick, counsel the troubled, and fulfill many of the duties formerly undertaken by traditional religious leaders. Robert Conkling's "Legitimacy and Conversion in Social Change: The Case of French Missionaries and the Northeastern Algonkian" [31] demonstrates this replacement role among the Abnaki. Jesuits enjoyed a freedom of movement and flexibility that Protestant workers, burdened with home and family, could never attain. The Catholic use of ceremony — processions, pictures, colorful vestments, impressive rites, and mysterious symbols — figured as another prominent point of difference. Sacramentalism gave Catholic missions an entrance into the Indian mental world and a functional purpose in the Indian daily world denied to Protestants. George C. Barker's "Some Functions of Catholic Processions in Pueblo and Yaqui Culture Change" [8], Florence Hawley's "The Role of Pueblo Social Organization in the Dissemination of Catholicism" [87], and Paul

Horgan's evocative biography of *Lamy of Santa Fe* [94] reveal the impact that Catholic affective ceremonies had on Indian life and mission success. Schooled in the tradition of preaching to a literate audience, Protestant missionaries discovered that their austere services had little appeal to those Indians whose traditional religions were grounded in ritual and group participation. They also found themselves handicapped by inadequate language training and lack of field support. They were often forced to rely on interpreters, frequently with some confusion in the translation. In the Blackfoot mission the language barrier so isolated the Methodists that most workers ultimately abandoned their missions to minister to congregations of white settlers. Most Catholic missionaries were armed with classical educations and extensive language training and were thus better able to develop Indian-language mission materials.

Anglican and Episcopal Missions

In 1680 Morgan Godwin, an Anglican clergyman, published a fiery pamphlet entitled *The Negro's and Indians Advocate* [75]. Godwin was furious with American Anglicans for failing to evangelize their "heathen" slaves and Indian neighbors. He hoped that his advocacy would inspire the needed efforts, but he was sorely disappointed. Not until the turn of the century did Anglicans begin to seek nonwhite converts.

Usually they did so under the auspices of the Society for the Propagation of the Gospel. In the years before the

Revolution, the SPG appointed several hundred missionaries for the colonies, but only a handful worked among Indians. The Society's Indian efforts can be traced in a number of important documents. *Missionalia* [24] is a collection of mission papers published in 1727 by Thomas Bray, one of the founders of the SPG. In 1770 William Knox wrote *Three Tracts respecting the Conversion and Instruction of the Free Indians and Negroe Slaves* [119]. The earnest but ill-fated efforts of one Anglican missionary are described in *The Carolina Chronicle of Dr. Francis Le Jau, 1706–1717* [117], edited by Frank J. Klingberg. The perennial problems of inadequate financial support and profound Indian indifference to Anglican teachings are documented in two valuable articles: "Indian Education and Missions in Colonial Virginia," by W. Stitt Robinson, Jr. [164], and "The Established Virginia Church and the Conversion of Negroes and Indians, 1620–1760," by Jerome W. Jones [105].

Under the aegis of Indian Affairs Superintendent Sir William Johnson, Anglicanism gained an important foothold among the Iroquois of New York. Johnson enjoyed a unique — even legendary — relationship with many of the tribes. Husband of Molly Brant, a prominent clan matron, he was bound to the Mohawks in marriage as well as diplomacy. *The Papers of Sir William Johnson* [103] reveal how this adroit politician fostered mission activity for secular ends. His *Papers* also contain a wealth of Anglican mission material, much of it pertaining to the successful Mohawk congregation. John Wolfe Lydekker's *The Faithful Mohawks* [128] treats the mission in both its New York and Canadian phases. Still more can be learned about SPG missionaries by consulting portions of their letters reprinted in *Anglican Humanitarianism in Colonial New York*, by Frank J. Klingberg [116]. Gerald J. Goodwin's article "Christianity, Civilization, and the Savage" [76] notes the relationship between mission tactics and church politics and argues that Anglican demands for native culture change arose from some bitter political skirmishing within the church itself.

The War for Independence had a devastating impact on the Church of England in America. Anglican missionary activity, never very successful, ceased. Like so many other Loyalists, Indians in John Stuart's Mohawk congregation fled to Canada. The church itself was forced to undergo an anguished period of self-examination. In 1789 the new Protestant Episcopal Church in the United States emerged. In 1820 it in turn chartered a missionary society to reawaken and coordinate mission work. "Anglicanism among the Indians of Washington Territory," by Thomas E. Jessett [100], discusses the endeavors of John West, David T. Jones, and Herbert Beaver in the period 1820–30. "Civilization and Christianization of the Ojibways in Minnesota" is Henry B. Whipple's account of the mission work begun by James Breck just before the Civil War [200]. Bishop Whipple was one of the most influential Episcopal mission planners in the nineteenth century; his autobiography, *Lights and Shadows of a Long Episcopate* [199], touches on many themes in Indian mission history.

Three additional studies round out the picture of

Episcopal efforts. "The Episcopal Mission to the Dakotas," by K. Brent Woodruff [207], details the labors of Episcopalians among the Sioux from 1860 to 1898. "Bishop William Crane Gray's Mission to the Seminole Indians in Florida," by Harry A. Kersey and Donald E. Pullease [113], covers the period 1893–1914 and illuminates a much-neglected mission area. "Protestant Missionary Activity among the Navajo," by Michael J. Warner [193], describes the establishment of an important Indian hospital at Fort Defiance in 1897.

Baptist Missions

Not until after the War of 1812 did the Baptists begin organized Indian mission work. The efforts of Baptist missionaries in the 1820s are detailed in "Early Baptist Missionary Work among the Cherokees," by James W. Moffitt [141]. A book valuable for its broad treatment of institutional growth is *Baptist Missions among the American Indians*, by Carl C. Rister [163].

The best-known Baptist Indian missionary was Isaac McCoy. In 1823 this vigorous man conceived an ambitious plan to create an Indian country west of Missouri where Christian Indians might live a holy, civilized life on individual farms. McCoy believed that such a plan was the Indian's best hope, for it would protect him from the corrupting influences of civilization that had so often confounded the mission effort. McCoy's varied career as missionary, political activist, and publicist is an arresting one. George A. Schultz has written a fine biography of

McCoy in *An Indian Canaan: Isaac McCoy and the Vision of
an Indian State* [170]. McCoy's own account was published
in 1840 as the *History of Baptist Indian Missions* [132].

McCoy's ideal of a separate territory for Indians was
well intentioned, but many other white Americans found
the idea of Indian removal attractive for less admirable
reasons. It is ironic that the efforts of McCoy and other
like-minded missionaries helped pave the way for the
federal Removal policy of the 1830s, for that enterprise
proved to be anything but benign. For most Indians,
Removal meant incalculable misery. Natives who resisted
found themselves beaten or swindled, then deprived of
all legal recourse. Some resisters were rounded up and
detained in what can only be called concentration camps.
Cooperative Indians often fared no better, facing death
by starvation, disease, or exposure on the bitter westward
trek. The infamous Trail of Tears cost the Cherokee
people four thousand lives, at the rate of approximately
thirteen a day. Though many missionaries opposed Removal with considerable spirit and force, enough favored it to give the policy an air of Christian respect-
ability.

Catholic Missions

The centralized bureaucracy and dedicated religious
orders of the Catholic church enabled it to undertake
Indian mission programs on a scale few Protestant
churches could match. Moreover, Catholic missions enjoyed a stability unique in mission history. For an un-

forgettable glimpse of Catholic mission work in eastern
North America, no work rivals *The Jesuit Relations*, edited
by Reuben Gold Thwaites [180]. This fascinating
seventy-three volume collection contains a wealth of eth-
nographic detail recorded by the missionaries in their
contacts with dozens of tribes from Canada to Louisiana
in the seventeenth and eighteenth centuries.

There are a number of general histories of Catholic
missions east of the Mississippi. The various efforts of
Jesuits are detailed in *The Jesuits of the Middle United States*,
by Gilbert J. Garraghan [67], *History of the Catholic Missions
among the Indian Tribes of the United States, 1529–1854,* by
John Gilmary Shea [172], *The Iroquois and the Jesuits*, by
Thomas Donohue [41], and *The French Jesuits in Lower
Louisiana*, by Jean Delanglez [35]. John Tate Lanning's
The Spanish Missions of Georgia [121] traces the growth of a
major mission system in the borderland between the
English and Spanish colonies of the Southeast. An
archeological study entitled *Here They Once Stood*, by
Mark Boyd, Hale Smith, and John Griffin [21], relates
the story of Franciscan missions to the Apalachee Indians. The Apalachee mission system was so successful
that it stood second in importance only to Saint Augustine. It prospered until the early eighteenth century,
when invasions by Creeks and white South Carolinians
destroyed it. Many Apalachees were sold into slavery by
the invaders, but one Christian chief led some survivors
to the new French missions near Pensacola in 1718.

Two other east-coast surveys are worthy of mention.
French Catholic Missions in the Present-Day United States, by

Mary Doris Mulvey [143], covers mission activity between 1604 and 1791. Mary Celeste Leger's *The Catholic Indian Missions in Maine* [122] describes mission work from 1611 to 1820 in northern New England.

Most mission histories concern themselves with institutional growth and neglect the important culture-contact aspects of the mission. One happy exception is the journal of Father Anthony Maria Gachet, entitled "Five Years in America" [65]. Father Gachet was a Swiss Capuchin who worked among the Menominee Indians of Kenosha, Wisconsin, from 1859 to 1862. His diary details the day-to-day activities of his mission and notes the persistence of Menominee religious beliefs in the face of his most strenuous efforts to eradicate them.

Histories of the Southwest, California, and Pacific Northwest missions are numerous and varied. The best tribe-by-tribe survey of Catholic missions in the Southwest can be found in Edward H. Spicer's *Cycles of Conquest* [177]. A compilation entitled *Rules and Precepts of the Jesuit Missions of Northwestern New Spain* [155] offers some valuable seventeenth- and eighteenth-century documents on the conduct of Spanish missions. The introduction by Charles W. Polzer contains a perceptive analysis of mission terminology, organization, and methodology.

The publication in 1936 of Herbert E. Bolton's epic *Rim of Christendom* [19] marked the beginning of intensive historical study of missions in the Southwest. This landmark work is a life-and-times biography of Father Eusebio Francisco Kino, a remarkable Jesuit who was an explorer and agricultural innovator as well as a missionary to the Pimas. Bolton's efforts have been carried forward by several other scholars. Mission growth in the years after the death of Father Kino is the subject of John Augustine Donohue's *After Kino: Jesuit Missions in Northwestern New Spain 1711–1767* [40].John Kessell's careful reconstruction of the Jesuit mission station at Guevavi, entitled *Mission of Sorrows* [114], should serve as a model for other mission histories, for it treats the mission as an organic, institutional whole instead of focusing on the efforts of a single missionary.

Much has been written of the Spanish missions in California, but a substantial part of the literature has actually hindered our understanding of the effort there. Romantic images of whitewashed churches and gentle padres have often obscured mission realities. Zephyrin Engelhardt's massive four-volume compendium *The Missions and Missionaries of California* [54] manifests this regrettable tendency. Listing mission workers and offering capsule biographies of each is the major contribution of Maynard J. Geiger's *Franciscan Missionaries in Hispanic California, 1769–1848* [72]. Two books by Peter Masten Dunne, *Pioneer Black Robes on the West Coast* [47] and *Black Robes in Lower California* [48], are essential for understanding mission growth. Both of Dunne's books are traditional in concept, tending to overlook Indians while examining in detail the lives of the missionaries. More than any other scholar, Sherburne F. Cook changed the nature of California mission studies. His *The Conflict between the California Indian and White Civilization* [32] draws heavily on demographic evidence to illustrate the

Indian rejection of mission life and culture change. Chapter 4 of Cook's work, entitled "Negative Responses to the Mission Environment," analyzes Indian discontent, noting that at least one out of every twenty mission Indians successfully escaped from the padres. Indian actions and responses take their rightful place in the story of California missions in the writings of Martha Voght and George Harwood Phillips. Voght's "Shamans and Padres" [189] demonstrates the persistence of Indian religions within the mission. Phillips's "Indians and the Breakdown of the Spanish Mission System in California" [153] finds that oppressive mission conditions played as central a role in the failure of the system as did the Indians' rejection of Christianity.

Jesuit Pierre-Jean De Smet is the Northwest's best-known Catholic missionary. His arduous journeys and extensive mission programs are well documented in his *Life, Letters, and Travels* [36]. Clarence B. Bagley's *Early Catholic Missions in Old Oregon* [5] and A. M. Jung's *Jesuit Missions among the American Tribes of the Rocky Mountain Indians* [108] are of value for the chronological framework they provide. Work done in the Dakotas and Minnesota between 1818 and 1864 is concisely described in Mary Aquinas Norton, *Catholic Missionary Activities in the Northwest* [144]. An outstanding study that blends ethnography, military history, and diplomatic insight is *The Jesuits and the Indian Wars of the Northwest*, by Robert Ignatius Burns [26].

Long before any missionaries came to them, the Flathead Indians showed an interest in Catholic Christianity.

In 1840 the ubiquitous Father De Smet baptized six hundred Flathead converts — the most easily won, enthusiastic converts he would ever encounter in his long career. The Flatheads welcomed the Blackrobes so heartily because they believed them to be the bearers of powerful "medicine"; that is, good fortune. For a time the Indians remained impressed with their mentors, but in less than ten years most of them became disillusioned, even hostile. In 1850 the Jesuits departed. Richard Forbis's "The Flathead Apostasy" [62] should be read beside the personal account of missionary Gregory Mengarini, *Recollections of the Flathead Mission* [139].

The Bureau of Catholic Indian Missions was organized in 1874 to coordinate mission work with federal policy. This was a turbulent time for missionaries, but even more so for Indian peoples. Indians were invariably asked to bear the harsh effects of experimental policies "for their own good." Readers can investigate this sorry period by consulting Francis Paul Prucha's *American Indian Policy in Crisis* [156] and Peter J. Rahill's *The Catholic Indian Missions and Grant's Peace Policy* [157].

Methodist Missions

Modern students find it difficult to trace early Methodist mission ventures; too many beginning efforts, especially those of roving circuit riders, went unrecorded. Even the Methodists' own mission society (founded in 1820) was unaware of many of the activities of its missionaries. Nonetheless, Wade C. Barclay has gathered the available evidence and used it to compile his valuable two-volume *History of Methodist Missions* [6]. *Part One, Early American Methodism*, covers the period 1769 to 1844; *Part Two, The Methodist Church*, traces development from 1845 to 1939.

Like most other Protestant denominations, the Methodists established a Cherokee mission and were optimistic about its future. Mary T. Peacock plots the growth of that project in "Methodist Mission Work among the Cherokee Indians before the Removal" [148]. The Methodist Wyandot mission, which began shortly after the end of the War of 1812 with the work of black missionary John Stewart, is the subject of several works. Highly recommended is *Indian Missionary Reminiscences, Principally of the Wyandot Nation*, by Charles Elliott [52]. A companion piece is the more famous *History of the Wyandott Mission, at Upper Sandusky, Ohio* by James Bradley Finley [60]. Methodist missions in the Southwest have received too little attention. Thomas Harwood's *History of the New Mexico Spanish and English Missions of the Methodist Episcopal Church* [85] is a start. Harwood was a pioneer missionary laboring in nineteenth-century New Mexico. His endeavors are compared with those of other Protestant missionaries in Warner's useful survey, "Protestant Missionary Activity among the Navajo" [193].

The story of Methodist missions, indeed the story of any denomination's endeavors, encompasses the efforts of many different people, all of them individuals with their own distinctive personalities. We need to remember that missionaries had varying backgrounds, abilities, and

temperaments. The careers of two Methodist missionaries, George Copway and Jason Lee, are cases in point.
George Copway was an Ojibway chief who converted to
Methodism in his youth and became a zealous evangelist.
His autobiography. *The Life, History, and Travels of Kah-
ge-ga-gah-bowh* [33], details (and probably exaggerates)
his lively mission labors. Jason Lee's career, while equally
interesting, ran a very different course. Lee worked
among the Chinook Indians for ten years but failed to
win a single convert. Lee's story is told by Robert J.
Loewenberg in *Equality on the Oregon Frontier: Jason Lee
and the Methodist Mission, 1834–43* [124].

Moravian Missions

Through few in number, Moravian missionaries
made a large mark on the history of Indian missions in
America. General historians have traditionally granted
their work an unusual respect. Yet their story is far from
told, for a vast amount of material — much of it in
German — lies virtually unexplored in the Moravian
church archives at Bethlehem, Pennsylvania.

David Zeisberger and John Heckewelder dominated
the Moravian missions in the eighteenth century. These
missionaries dedicated their lives to the establishment
and maintenance of Christian Indian towns in Pennsylvania, Ohio, and Ontario. In that turbulent era of
Indian-white relations, their towns for a time sheltered
and sustained many Indian converts. The diaries of Zeisberger and Heckewelder are splendid mission records,
revealing the many roles (pastor, educator, farmer, doc-

tor, tradesman, and handyman) that a missionary had to play. *The Diary of David Zeisberger*, edited by Eugene F. Bliss [209], should be read with "David Zeisberger's Official Diary, Fairfield, 1791–1795," edited by Paul E. Mueller [210]. John Heckewelder's *A Narrative of the Mission of the United Brethren among the Delaware and Mohegan Indians* [88] should be read in conjunction with the parts of his travel diaries printed in *Thirty-Thousand Miles with John Heckewelder*, edited by Paul A. W. Wallace [89]. These and other documents were used to good effect by Elma and Leslie Gray, whose *Wilderness Christians* [80] tells the story of the Moravian mission to the Delawares.

More than any other missionaries, the Moravians came to know tragedy. They learned that the white man's racism could doom the mission as surely as the Indian's resistance. Even Christianized, politically neutral Indians made convenient scapegoats for white zealots who literally believed that the only good Indian is a dead Indian. In 1782 such sentiments culminated in the brutal murder of ninety-six Delaware Christians (including many women, children, and old men) at the Moravian village of Gnadenhütten. This was the greatest atrocity of the American Revolution, but no white militiaman was ever officially censured for taking part in it. Although Heckewelder was away at the time of the massacre, his *Narrative* contains a chilling account, based upon the testimony of several eyewitnesses. The Gnadenhütten disaster forced the surviving Delaware Christians to flee the country. With the help of the missionaries, they reestablished their village at Fairfield, Ontario. Unlike so many other efforts, the Moravian missions were doomed largely by assaults from without, not by weaknesses within.

George H. Loskiel's *History of the Mission of the United Brethren among the Indians in North America* [125] and Edmund Schwarze's *History of the Moravian Missions among the Southern Indian Tribes of the United States* [171] offer the "official" church view of missions but are indispensable surveys nonetheless. The various activities and problems of one early mission are detailed in *Moravian Journals relating to Central New York, 1745–66*, edited by William M. Beauchamp [12]. A short-lived (1801–06) but important Moravian project in Indiana is described in the *The Moravian Indian Mission on White River*, a rich set of documents edited by Lawrence Henry Gipson [74]. An essay entitled "The Moravian Mission to the American Indians," by Thomas F. McHugh [133], describes the distinctive "Peace Corps" character of the Moravian approach. Kenneth G. Hamilton's "Cultural Contributions of Moravian Missions among the Indians" [82] notes the emphasis given Bible study, hymnody, orderliness, and industry in mission villages.

Mormon Missions

It is unfortunate that students of Indian missions have tended to ignore Mormon activities, for they are among the most interesting. Mormon missionaries used the same methods as other mission workers and were motivated by many of the same impulses, but many aspects of the Mormon mission story are unique. The Mormons preached a *new* religion, one that gave Indians a special place within it. They assumed that Native Americans were the "Lamanites" described by Joseph Smith in the *Book of Mormon* and constituted one of the "lost tribes of Israel." The "Lamanites" had fallen from grace and become "a dark and loathsome people." Mormon missionaries were certain that faith and civilization would make them "white and delightsome" again. Not by chance, Utah Mormons preferred to have "civilized" Indians for neighbors as a buffer between themselves and less friendly tribes. Ever threatened by the prospect of federal action against them for the practice of polygamy, the beleaguered Mormons were especially eager to make converts who would be friends and allies as well.

"The First Mormon Mission to the Indians," by Warren A. Jennings [99], describes work done among some Delawares living in Kansas in the 1830s. Here the Mormons were able to build upon existing Delaware beliefs, proclaiming Mormonism to be the fulfillment of all the traditional rites. As a result of this syncretism a number of Delawares converted, to the dismay of nearby Protestant missionaries. Ultimately, denominational rivalries forced the Mormons to withdraw from the Kansas mission arena.

One Mormon's labors are recorded in the *Journal of the Southern Indian Mission*: *Diary of Thomas D. Brown*, edited by Juanita Brooks [25]. Another important missionary was Jacob Hamblin, who worked among the

Hopis. The Indians welcomed the agricultural and technological innovations he proposed but wanted no part of his religious teachings. Hamblin's career is traced in "The Hopis and the Mormons, 1858–1873," by Charles S. Peterson [149].

Mormon missionaries were more successful with the Shoshonis of Idaho, Utah, and Wyoming. A valuable article by Lawrence G. Coates entitled "Mormons and Social Change among the Shoshoni, 1853–1900" [29] describes the long Mormon involvement with the tribe. Shoshoni responses to Mormonism and its civilization program varied with changing circumstances. In the 1870s and 1880s many Shoshonis embraced the new religion to help them cope with reservation life. Others converted because they wanted to escape the system altogether. Many Shoshoni converts came to the town of Washakie near Salt Lake City. Under Mormon direction, convert families learned white skills and values. Washakie proved to be a durable enterprise, lasting as an identifiable Indian town well into the present century. Later Mormon efforts within the federal reservation system were not nearly as successful.

Navajo responses to Mormon missionizing are noted in "Changing Navajo Religious Values," by Robert N. Rapoport [158]. This anthropological field study compares the Mormon mission with that of a certain unnamed evangelical group. Despite the use of fictitious names for people and places, the study is a valuable source of culture-contact material.

Presbyterian and American Board Missions

The Presbyterian contribution to Indian mission history was rich and varied. A colonial Presbyterian mission project is described by Samuel C. Williams in "An Account of the Presbyterian Mission to the Cherokee, 1757–1759" [203]. The early nineteenth century work of one notable missionary is analyzed in "Gideon Blackburn's Mission to the Cherokees," by Dorothy C. Bass [10]. Blackburn introduced the ideas of boarding schools and constitutional government to the Cherokees.

In 1810 Indian mission history entered a vital new phase with the creation of the American Board of Commissioners for Foreign Missions. This interdenominational Protestant society soon became largely a "new school" Presbyterian agency. Between 1812 and 1865 it supported more Indian missionaries — and maintained more complete records — than any other mission organization. *The Story of the American Board*, by William E. Strong [178], recalls one hundred years of board missions. *Sketches of the Mission of the American Board*, published in 1872 by Samuel Colcord Bartlett [9], relates work done among the Creeks, Cherokees, Chickasaws, and Sioux. Though excessively congratulatory at times, Bartlett's work is valuable. His poignant account of Southern Indian Removal is not easily forgotten. Succinct and well written, it describes the role of board missionaries Elizur Butler and Samuel Worcester. Both were imprisoned in Georgia for their resistance to Indian Removal. In 1832 their appeals brought about the historic Supreme Court case *Worcester* v. *Georgia*. When the court ruled in Worcester's favor, both Georgia and President Jackson ignored the finding. Removal proceeded, and a number of board missionaries followed their charges into Indian Territory.

The efforts of three pioneer board missionaries are detailed in "The Lac Qui Parle Indian Mission," by Charles M. Gates [68]. T. S. Williamson, Stephen R. Riggs, and Gideon Pond administered this troubled mission with varying degrees of success from 1835 to 1854 among the Wah-peton Sioux of the Minnesota Territory. Stephen Riggs, one of the ablest board missionaries in the trans-Mississippi West, wrote two important books based on his experiences. *Tah-koo-wah-kań* [161] and *Mary and I; or, Forty Years with the Sioux* [162] are compelling personal accounts that illuminate both mission practices and Indian reactions.

Board activities have been analyzed in a number of other works. An essay by Harold Hickerson, "William T. Boutwell of the American Board and the Pillager Chippewa" [91], characterizes that enterprise as "a failure." A more optimistic view of Chippewa work is reflected in *Notices of Chippeway Converts* by board missionary William Montague Ferry [58]. Ferry's own mission correspondence has been partially reprinted in "Frontier Mackinac Island, 1823–1834" [59]. The tortured relations between the board and its distant Whitman mission are traced in *Marcus and Narcissa Whitman and the Opening of Old Oregon* [46], by Clifford Merrill

Drury. It was the sudden end of the Whitman mission in 1847 that persuaded the board to abandon its efforts in the Pacific Northwest. Two other books by Clifford Drury are also valuable for the Northwest. *Henry Harmon Spalding: Pioneer of Old Oregon* [44] should be read with *The Diaries and Letters of Henry H. Spalding and Asa Bowen Smith relating to the Nez Perce Mission, 1838–1842* [45].

Despite the efforts of its many missionaries, American Board Indian missions reaped "little else than disappointment." In *Protestant America and the Pagan World* [152], Clifton J. Phillips quotes these words from an 1838 board report to summarize the agency's feelings after a generation of costly activity. Phillip's account of Indian missions is brief but valuable. It discusses the earliest board endeavors, the ardent anti-Removal crusade of Secretary Jeremiah Evarts, and the character of the ill-fated Whitman mission. All of these are placed in the context of the board's international missions. Robert F. Berkhofer's *Salvation and the Savage* [16] also treats the board's missions with insight. The *Missionary Herald,* the official periodical of the board, is filled with Indian mission reports, often edited to remove tales of discouragement and Indian opposition.

In the years before the Civil War, Presbyterian and American Board missionaries were deeply divided on the issue of slavery. Both in the pre-Removal South and later in Indian Territory, many Cherokee and Choctaw families owned slaves. A substantial number of missionaries were opposed to continuing mission work among those tribes as long as slavery persisted. Two essays by William G. McLoughlin, "Indian Slaveholders and Presbyterian Missionaries, 1837–1861" [134] and "The Choctaw Slave Burning: A Crisis in Mission Work among the Indians" [136], are perceptive analyses of that complex problem. Also of value is Robert T. Lewitt's "Indian Missions and Anti-Slavery Sentiment" [123].

Quaker Missions

The Friends did not actively seek Indian converts, for they believed that Christian conversion was a private matter, made possible by the "inner light" already possessed by every person. Quaker mission work was thus characterized by humanitarian, not evangelical concerns. Rayner Wickersham Kelsey's *Friends and Indians* [112] is the best general account of Quaker activities from 1655 to 1917. Also valuable is the nineteenth-century document *Some Account of the Conduct of the Religious Society of Friends towards the Indian Tribes . . . of East and West Jersey and Pennsylvania* [64].

The Death and Rebirth of the Seneca, by Anthony F. C. Wallace [192], discusses the important role the Friends played in the life of this Iroquois tribe after the American Revolution. By 1796 the Quaker Indian Committee had developed a thoroughgoing Seneca "civilization" plan designed to transform their "slums in the wilderness" into more habitable American-style towns. Wallace notes that the Friends succeeded in bringing vital technical assistance to a large number of Eastern Indians. The work of Halliday Jackson, one of the Seneca missionaries, is described in his first-person account *Civilization of the Indian Natives* [97].

The so-called Quaker Peace Policy of President U. S. Grant is perhaps the Quakers' most notable contribution to the story of Indian missions. Quakers were among those Protestants most active in urging Indian policy reform on President Grant. In 1869 Quakers succeeded in persuading Grant to appoint missionaries as Indian agents. This new policy transferred the control of Indian affairs from the secular (often military) sphere to the religious and gave thirteen different denominations a free hand on their respective reservations. Francis Paul Prucha's *American Indian Policy in Crisis* [156] describes the "Peace Policy" and explains why it failed, despite the high hopes of its advocates.

Goals of the Mission

From the beginning of the mission enterprise until well into the present century, missionary rhetoric — Catholic and Protestant — proclaimed one goal: to save the immortal souls of lost Indians from eternal damnation. But even the most otherworldly missionaries quickly recognized that conversion of the Indian soul was insufficient. The conquest had to be more complete. A radical change in the Indian body — in all aspects of appearance and conduct — was also required. Missionaries were very much a part of, indeed leaders of, Euro-American culture — a culture that blended Christianity and Western ways into a potent culture-religion. In the missionary perspective, Indians could not be Christians until they first abandoned native habits and accepted "civilized" customs. Conversion meant both the invasion of the Indian body and the conquest of the Indian soul. In nearly every mission these two distinct but interrelated goals were operative. Indians were urged to abandon their "wild" ways and become sanitized Euro-Americans. In many instances they were also forced to give up land and political autonomy. "Civilization and salvation" was the credo of nearly every North American missionary, which often proved to be a euphemism for cultural invasion and tribal decline.

In *Salvation and the Savage* [16], Robert F. Berkhofer describes the civilization and salvation formula. "Most other Americans wanted only minor changes in Indian customs," he writes (p. 106), "but the missionaries sought nothing less than a revolution in social relations and basic values." The insistence on radical social change as an essential mission goal can be traced through the writings of many prominent mission workers. One of the concept's most ardent proponents was the New England Puritan John Eliot. "I find it absolutely necessary to carry on civility with religion," he stressed (*Colls. Mass. His. Soc.*, 3d ser., 4 [1834]: 88). As William Kellaway explains in *The New England Company, 1649–1776* [110], Eliot's civilization arguments marked the beginning of a long mission tradition in the Northeast.

As missions proliferated after the American Revolution, the civilization goal remained an integral part of mission ideology. Nineteenth-century missionaries, products of an intensely nationalistic culture, defined civilization as a mixture of sedentary agriculture, individualism, capitalism, and routine labor. Earlier missionaries had expressed their strong personal preference for changes in dress, hair style, language, and sexual behavior. In the nineteenth century those changes were elevated to matters of faith and dogma. Missionaries set higher standards of conduct for their Indian converts than for their fellow Americans. "The Choctaw Mission," by Dawson A. Phelps [151], explores the use of formal schooling in the pre-Removal period to promote the acceptance of Euro-American ways. Edward H. Spicer's *Cycles of Conquest* [177] illustrates the growth of the civilization idea in the Southwest from the Spanish mission to the present. Perhaps the best extended analysis of mission goals among one tribe is Howard L. Harrod's *Mission among the Blackfeet* [84]. Harrod explains that though there were some differences between the Methodists' and the Jesuits' views of civilization, both groups required the Blackfeet to renounce their traditional culture.

While laboring to "civilize" the Indians, missionaries frequently promoted the secular designs of empire and state. "Missionaries showed little regard for Indian cultures while advancing the cultural values and, often, the political goals of the conquerors," writes Neal Salisbury in "Red Puritans" [167, p. 28]. Francis Jennings makes a similar point in "Goals and Functions of Puritan Missions to the Indians" [98]. In Eliot's mission, for example, missionaries strove to undermine tribal leadership by dividing Indians into Christian and traditionalist factions. Missionaries and their converts mocked the prominent shamans, belittled traditional rites and ceremonies, and weakened the authority of sachems — all at the time when the native peoples of southern New England desperately needed tribal unity in the face of English invasion. Another clear example of missionary interests merging with those of the state can be seen in Francis Paul Prucha's *American Indian Policy in Crisis* [156]. In the name of civilization, Christian reformers gave support to the Dawes Act of 1887 and similar legislation aimed at furthering the expansionist policies of the federal government. Such support was neither malicious nor conspiratorial in intent, but was based on the firm conviction that Indians could not take on the substance of Christian faith until they had accepted the forms of American civilization.

Methods of Conversion

Mission Towns

Missionaries sought to develop environments that would foster the double goals of the mission. They believed that these environments should feature all the familiar Euro-American institutions: monogamous family, sedentary agriculture, civil government, formal education, and organized churches. At the heart of their plans lay the town ideal. Because the life of the town was so much a part of how Europeans defined civilization, missionaries quickly seized upon the concept of building convert towns. These "praying towns" or "reductions" would be orderly Christian communities filled with model converts, all living and working under the watchful eye of the priest or pastor. One of the earliest expositions of the mission town concept appears in Father Paul Le Jeune's "Annual Relation of Events in New France, 1634," printed in *The Jesuit Relations* [180, pp. 6-7]. As Le Jeune noted, mission towns were designed to do more than give converts new identities and allegiances. Towns would also serve to isolate the converts from their unconverted kinsmen, thus preventing the kind of reversion to traditional belief all missionaries feared. As an added benefit, towns would conserve mission manpower while increasing the influence of the missionaries-in-residence. These benefits and more were anticipated by the missionaries as well as by governmental officials, who were quick to recognize the town's value as a means of controlling Indian people.

In southern New England John Eliot and his co-workers established a sizable network of praying towns. Before being swept away by King Philip's War, fourteen praying towns harbored a population of some 1,100 natives. In "Red Puritans," Neal Salisbury offers a penetrating analysis of the towns and their place in Eliot's mission scheme. Salisbury observes that Eliot's town regulations were tantamount to demanding that "Indians no longer be Indians" [167, p. 54]. Eliot's showcase town was

Natick, founded in 1651. With buildings and streets laid out in English style, Natick was to be the model for other Indian Christian communities. Some important information about daily life in Natick and its economic activities can be found in two contemporary accounts by Massachusetts's superintendent of Indian affairs, Daniel Gookin: "An Historical Account of the Doings and Sufferings of the Christian Indians in New England" [78] and "Historical Collections of the Indians in New England" [77].

In the eighteenth and early nineteenth centuries, Moravian missionaries in the Old Northwest built a similar set of towns for the same purposes. Villages such as Schönbrunn, Gnadenhütten, and the White River post in Indiana were all designed to civilize and evangelize various tribal peoples. While much has been said about the noncoercive tactics of the Moravians, a careful look at town regulations and daily village life reveals a unity of purpose with the more authoritarian dreams of John Eliot. A careful reading of *The Diary of David Zeisberger* [209] and *Indian Mission on White River* [74] indicates that the Moravians required nearly as much culture change from their potential converts as did other missionaries.

Spanish missions in the Southwest and California also utilized the town idea as a major means to cultural and spiritual conversion. Donohue's *After Kino* [40], Kessell's *Mission of Sorrows* [114], and Spicer's *Cycles of Conquest* [177] provide an introduction to the many mission towns of the Southwest. The institutional development of mission settlements in Hispanic California is fully traced in

Englehardt's *The Missions and Missionaries of California* [54]. For a fuller perspective on culture contact, Cook's *Conflict between the California Indian and White Civilization* [32] should be consulted. Of special importance is Voght's "Shamans and Padres" [189]. This valuable article describes how Indian religions survived within the mission that despised them, giving spiritual sustenance to many Indian townspeople.

Institutional Education

Missionaries, from the sixteenth century on, believed that the school, like the town and the church, should be employed as a major weapon in the struggle for Indian minds, souls, and bodies. Most missionaries were certain that Indians had the intellectual capabilities to master the Western arts and sciences and hence to fully grasp Christian teachings. They were convinced that what was needed was a learning environment that would cut Indians off from their tribal values and redirect their minds along Euro-American paths. Curriculum and teaching methods varied widely, depending on the abilities of teachers and the extent of support. Like other contemporary schools, mission schools were influenced by prevailing educational theories, moving in one generation from classical studies to vocational training and back again. Some schools concentrated on Bible study, while others hammered away at basic literacy. Most gave English-language instruction the highest priority. Students were often prohibited from, and sometimes punished for, speaking tribal languages, because the missionaries realized that Indian languages perpetuated Indian cultures. Within many schools, mission teachers sought to prepare converts for the demands of the Euro-American economic order by teaching agricultural, technical, and domestic trades. Day schools were most common in frontier areas. The boarding school approach was used with increasing frequency as Indian populations shrank. Both missionaries and government agents favored the boarding-school method since it gave them more control over the lives of Indian students. Nearly every mission teacher craved to teach in such a controlled environment, for the immense task of cultural transformation was a round-the-clock effort. Indian mission education existed wholly to remake Indians in the "civilized"image. Nineteenth-century photographs tell the story: short-haired Indian children, scrubbed and manicured, sit attentively in tidy classroom rows. They were exposed to a medium that was its own message. If Indian parents rejected civilization, so argued mission teachers, then surely their children could be made to wear trousers and dresses, farm the land, read English, and serve the Christian God.

Mission education in the English colonies was a rather haphazard undertaking. Few bilingual teachers and limited financial resources gave the enterprise a ragtag appearance. Education in the Eliot mission was intensely catechetical and classical, and it produced the Indian assistants who helped translate Eliot's famous *Indian Bible*. Norman E. Tanis has written of "Education in John

Eliot's Indian Utopias" [179], but he does not sufficiently analyze the impact of European education on Indians. The rather meager efforts at Indian education in Virginia are explored in "Indian Education and Mission in Colonial Virginia," by W. Stitt Robinson [164]. Frank J. Klingberg's "Early Attempts at Indian Education in South Carolina" [118] is useful for another southern colony. Perhaps the most typical educational enterprise of the colonial era was Moor's Indian Charity School in Connecticut. Under the ambitious guidance of Eleazar Wheelock, the school enjoyed a short fame before withering and being moved into the shadow of Dartmouth College in New Hampshire. A telltale glimpse of daily student life there is provided by *The Letters of Eleazar Wheelock's Indians*, edited by James Dow McCallum [129]. These unusually frank letters reveal the cultural alienation experienced by many of the students. Wheelock's own ideas on Indian education and his efforts to create and promote the school can be followed in the *Continuations* of his *A Plain and Faithful Narrative* [198]. The most recent biography of Wheelock is McCallum's *Eleazar Wheelock, Founder of Dartmouth College* [130].

The best general introduction to the Protestant mission schools of the nineteenth century is contained in Berkhofer's *Salvation and the Savage* [16]. Drawing largely on the experience of the American Board of Commissioners for Foreign Missions, Berkhofer discusses study content, discipline, problems of attendance, and parental opposition to American education. The manner in which individual denominations and missionaries organized their schools is revealed in studies such as "Gideon Blackburn's Mission to the Cherokees," by Bass [10], "Early Baptist Missionary Work among the Cherokees," by Moffitt [141], and *Bringing the Gospel in Hogan and Pueblo*, by Dolfin [37]. The latter work needs to be supplemented by two essays by Michael J. Warner: "The Fertile Ground: The Beginnings of Protestant Missionary Work with the Navajos, 1852–1890" [194] and "Protestant Missionary Activity among the Navajo, 1890–1912" [193]. American Board missionary Stephen R. Riggs had much to say about the resistance of Indian parents to the culture change promoted by mission schools. Riggs's most important book, *Tah-koo-wah-kan*, [161], contains much information on absenteeism, language problems, and discipline. Martha B. Caldwell has edited the *Annals of Shawnee Methodist Mission and Indian Manual Labor School* [27], which provide insight into that Methodist experiment in vocational training.

Catholic mission schools enjoyed some important advantages over their Protestant counterparts. Catholic schools could rely on the services of trained priests and teaching sisters, and draw from a longer tradition of religious education. In *Attitudes of Missionary Sisters toward American Indian Acculturation* [160], Frances Mary Riggs points out that the schools could depend on a cadre of highly skilled and deeply motivated teachers. Dominic B. Gerlach's "St. Joseph's Indian Norman School, 1888–1896" [73] describes a Catholic boarding school for native teachers in Indiana. Catholic mission schools also sprouted up along Minnesota Territory's Red River in

1818. These schools are discussed by Hugh Graham in "Catholic Missionary Schools among the Indians of Minnesota" [79]. Mission education was opposed there, as elsewhere, by parents concerned about the loss of traditional culture and by fur traders who were convinced that the agricultural message in mission teaching would undermine their business. A chronicle of school growth in South Dakota to 1935 is provided by M. Serena Zens in "The Educational Work of the Catholic Church among the Indians of South Dakota" [211]. Bruce Rubenstein's "To Destroy a Culture: Indian Education in Michigan, 1855–1900" [166] narrates the change in that state from Catholic boarding schools to federal day schools. Typical of the larger Catholic reservation establishments was the Holy Family Mission School for the Blackfeet. Harrod's *Mission among the Blackfeet* [84] discusses it and its impact on the tribe and reproduces some photographs of the extensive mission buildings. A useful review of Catholic mission education in the Southwest can be found in Mary Stanislaus Van Well's *The Educational Aspects of the Missions in the Southwest* [183].

It is unfortunate that most mission school studies neglect to record the sentiments of Indian students. One book stands with McCallum's *Letters of Eleazar Wheelock's Indians* [129] as a powerful account of student life. *The Middle Five: Indian Schoolboys of the Omaha Tribe*, by Francis La Flesche [120], describes the experiences of pupils at a Presbyterian mission school in northeastern Nebraska during the 1860s.

Indian Churches

Ultimately, missionaries hoped to bring civilized Indians together into churches or congregations. Like the school and the town, the church was to serve as a place for both spiritual nurture and cultural change. Historians and anthropologists have not studied Indian churches carefully, and the available information usually takes the form of mission reports that sometimes suffer from inflated statistics and a "body count" mentality.

While there is a dearth of material for many churches, we do have a number of helpful works relating to John Eliot's Indian congregations. Eliot's two accounts, *Tears of Repentance* [51] and *A Late and Further Manifestation of the Progress of the Gospel amongst the Indians in New-England* [50], include confessions of faith made by praying-town converts and reveal much of the character of the Indian churches. Salisbury discusses the question of admission to church membership in these congregations in "Red Puritans" [167].

Like Eliot, Thomas Mayhew included Indian testimonies of faith in his writings. *Tears of Repentance* [51] contains Mayhew's report on the missions of Martha's Vineyard, which are also described in *Thomas Mayhew, Patriarch to the Indians*, by Lloyd C. M. Hare [83]. Thomas's grandson Experience compiled *Indian Converts* [138], a remarkable book containing the capsule biographies of the Mayhew mission's most exemplary Christians. Berkhofer's *Salvation and the Savage* [16] contains an illuminating chapter on Indian congregations, with examples drawn from many denominations. Harrod's

Mission among the Blackfeet [84] compares Jesuit and Methodist concepts of the Indian church.

Indian Responses

Both clerical and lay historians have accepted at face value the notion that what is important in mission history are the missionaries, their actions, and their ideas. Indians have usually been portrayed as passive children or unthinking opponents of an obviously superior religion. A careful reading of the evidence dispels this illusion. Indians were not merely acted upon; they were actors. Their words and deeds affected mission history as surely as the missionaries' did.

Native Americans displayed a wide range of responses. Some welcomed the missionary message and became converts, while others criticized what they saw as a senseless, alien ideology. Many Indians coped with change by incorporating Christian elements into their lives. A number participated in revitalization movements. Still others chose to repel the mission by force.

Conversion

In spite of considerable opposition, missionaries did make sizable numbers of converts. Their efforts yielded many Indian preachers, as well as lay readers and assistants. Missionaries working in places where there had been considerable Indian-white intermarriage gained most of their converts from the children of such unions. In fact, several missions existed largely to minister to persons of mixed heritage. Missionary reports and memoirs contain especially rich material on Indian converts and their lives. While this information is often filled with hagiographic stereotypes, careful study of the documents can yield important insights into convert life. *The Jesuit Relations* [180], Mayhew's *Indian Converts* [138], and the Eliot tracts [49, 50, 51] contain striking narratives of conversion.

Nineteenth-century missionary journals are also filled with conversion narratives. The *Missionary Herald,* published in Boston by the American Board, is an excellent source, as is *Notices of Chippeway Converts*, by American Board missionary William M. Ferry [58].

Only a few Indian converts wrote extensively about their own experiences. Perhaps the best-documented early convert was Samson Occom, an eighteenth-century Mohegan preacher and teacher who studied under and later worked with Eleazar Wheelock. His biography is told in Harold Blodgett's *Samson Occom* [17] and in Leon Burr Richardson's edition of letters entitled *An Indian Preacher in England* [159]. Another notable convert-author was William Apes, a Pequot Indian born in 1798 and later adopted by the Mashpee tribe. Apes wrote *The Experiences of Five Christian Indians of the Pequod Tribe* [3] and an autobiography, *A Son of the Forest* [2]. George Copway, a nineteenth-century Chippewa chief who became an ardent Methodist missionary, related his conversion experience in *The Life, History and Travels of Kah-ge-ga-gah-bowh* [33]. Copway's *Life* contains vivid descriptions of Indian conversions experienced at mass revival meetings.

Though the historical evidence for the study of Indian converts is large, scholars have largely failed to analyze that evidence systematically. Those writing in the tradition of missionary apologetics have viewed conversion as an act of God, while those less sympathetic to the spiritual goals of the mission have dismissed Indian converts as merely "rice Christians." Berkhofer has suggested that "not a few converts gathered about the mission to share the 'loaves and fishes' more than the blood of Christ" [16:114]. But certainly there were many Native Americans who testified to the power of the gospel in their lives. Mission historians cannot dismiss these genuine converts. For each different mission situation at least two questions should be asked: How many converts embraced Christianity in earnest? How many merely acquiesced when resistance no longer made sense? Only with answers to these basic questions can we begin to appreciate the role of conversion in Indian life. John F. Freeman's flawed essay "The Indian Convert" [63] suggests how much work remains to be done in this area. Fruitful approaches to the problems of native conversion can be found in many recent studies of African and Asian missions.

Indian Theological Criticism of the Mission

Mission literature is dotted with important Indian observations that have long been overlooked. Much of the Indian comment is in the form of searching and often pointed questions directed at missionaries. Such queries show that Indians possessed a solid understanding of their own spiritual categories and were able to question those of others. The questions found in the Eliot tracts and *The Jesuit Relations* range over matters of sin, death, social ethics, and biblical interpretation. In "We Are Well as We Are" [165] James Ronda uses this arresting native evidence to demonstrate that missionaries and Indians engaged in rigorous theological debates.

Throughout the history of missions in North America, one Indian response appears repeatedly. Jesuits working in New France early in the seventeenth century were told "your world is different from ours; the God who created yours did not create ours" [180,–2:7-9]. Centuries later, Protestant missionaries attempting to convert Navajos encountered the same reply. "All different tribes have their own religion," reasoned one Navajo, "so you can keep your own religion and I can keep my own religion too" [158:86]. Most Indians professed belief in this "two ways" or "two roads" philosophy. They argued that religious beliefs and rituals were culture-bound and could not be exported to other cultures. This brand of cultural relativism left many missionaries nonplussed and effectively reinforced traditional beliefs. Similar kinds of criticism are recorded in "Documents relating to the Stockbridge Mission, 1825–48," edited by Thwaites [181]. McLoughlin's "Cherokee Anti-Mission Sentiment" [135], and Harrod's *Mission among the Blackfeet* [84] also contain memorable Indian criticisms.

Syncretism

Faced with the physical and political demands of an increasingly Euro-American world, substantial numbers of Indians mixed indigenous theologies and Christian symbols to create the religious experience anthropologists call syncretism. Indians gave traditional meanings to Christian rites, dogmas, and saints, thus insuring native cultural survival. Syncretism has been extensively studied by scholars of the mission outside North America, but similar research for North American missions is only now being undertaken. Edward P. Dozier's "Spanish-Catholic Influences on Rio Grande Pueblo Religion" [43], Paul H. Ezell's *The Hispanic Acculturation of the Gila River Pimas* [55], and Voght's "Shamans and Padres" [189] suggest the interior survival of tradition. It is difficult to determine the extent of syncretism in the colonial New England missions. Salisbury argues that the inhabitants of the praying towns may have found traditional meanings in the public acts of Christian worship such as Bible-reading and group hymn-singing. In "Legitimacy and Conversion in Social Change" [31], Conkling observes that over time the Jesuits became the functional substitute for traditional Abnaki shamans.

Revitalization

Missionaries claimed that Christianity and "civilization" could dramatically transform Indians into new moral creatures. Faith, they believed, could revitalize dead Indian souls, making them live again for the Christian God. Some anthropologists agree that Christianity itself became a powerful revitalization force for many Indian peoples. Cherokee Baptists, Huron Catholics, and Sioux Episcopalians all found in convert Christianity new sources of spiritual strength that helped them cope with their rapidly changing world.

But some Indians participated in another kind of re-vitalization — one that took missionaries by surprise. In several different regions revitalization religions emerged to compete with the white man's creeds. These Indian-centered religions usually featured a native prophet or charismatic figure who warned the Indians to reaffirm their ancient beliefs before it was too late. Most contained identifiably Christian elements while clearly rejecting Christianity itself. One such movement centered on the Seneca prophet Handsome Lake. In *Death and Rebirth of the Seneca* [192], Wallace describes the events surround-ing the movement and its impact on the Seneca. After a series of visions, Handsome Lake combined traditional Iroquois values with those learned from Quaker mission workers to compose an ethical code emphasizing those virtues — old and new — that were to bring about a renaissance of nineteenth-century Iroquois culture.

Handsome Lake's variety of revitalization was essen-tially positive. It implied a measure of respect for parts of the mission message. But many other revitalization reli-gions rejected nearly all Christian or Euro-American elements. *The Jesuit Relations* [180] include a number of such negative movements. In the 1640s several revitaliza-tion prophets enjoined the Hurons to return to their ancient practices and to shun French trade goods and mission teachings. One Huron related that Iouskeha, the Master of Life, had appeared to him in a vision. Iouskeha denounced the missionaries and chastised the Huron for neglecting their traditional rites. Similar examples of revitalization in more recent times include the teachings of the prophet Wovoka and the Ghost Dance religion, the peyote cult, and the rise of the Native American Church.

Armed Resistance

As conversion represents one end of the spectrum of Indian responses, armed resistance represents the other. Wherever tribal peoples maintained political autonomy, the forcible ejection or execution of the missionaries was always a possibility. Indians usually rejected such radical alternatives because the mission seemed to pose no immediate threat. In fact, the presence of mission workers often meant continued trade contacts and other benefits. Deeply ingrained values of hospitality also deterred Indians from resorting to such harsh measures. However, the alternative was there, and at times the decision was made to employ it. As much of the mission literature emphasizes, Indian missions yielded a number of grisly martyrdoms. Most histories have dealt with such events by eulogizing the victims and reviling their executioners. The accounts that describe the deaths of Jesuit Father Jogues or Marcus and Narcissa Whitman, for example, contain far more hagiography than history. They seldom explore the causes of the violence. One exception is Bowden's "Spanish Missions, Cultural Conflict and the Pueblo Revolt of 1680" [20], which analyzes Indian and missionary roles in mission history's bloodiest episode.

Conclusion

The missionaries to the North American Indians embarked upon their tasks with boundless enthusiasm and determination. The seventeenth-century Jesuit Paul Le Jeune expressed his optimism in a letter to a fellow Frenchman. "The road to Heaven seems shorter and surer from our great forests than from your large cities," he wrote [180,–18:85]. Two and a half centuries later, Cocia Hartog, a Protestant mission teacher working with the Navajo, wrote confidently that "the future of the Navajo is promising" [37:371]. But the same missionaries who began with such elevated hopes soon discovered that most Indians displayed either studied indifference or open hostility to the Christian mission. In the battle for Indian souls, victory was always elusive. At day's end, many mission workers wondered whether their labors would ever bear fruit.

And yet they seldom admitted defeat. Driven by the need to demonstrate the success of Christianity, they filled their public writings with optimistic predictions. Missionary literature betrayed a "body count" mentality. Indian converts were totted up on the abacus of faith and duly reported in letters, sermons, and denominational periodicals. It would be a serious mistake to proclaim the mission a success on the basis of these glowing, often inflated, and ultimately meaningless statistics. On the other hand, to pronounce the mission a failure because it often destroyed the integrity of native culture would also be a mistake. We might best evaluate a mission by judging its performance, goal by goal. How well did missionaries succeed in changing Indians to fit Christian European models? How effective was their campaign to convince Indians of the necessity of "civilized" Christian conversion? Finally, how successful were the missionaries in undermining Indian cultures so as to create a crisis in which it would be necessary for the Indians to seek "Christian civility" as a solution? These questions allow us to avoid the "numbers game" and still make meaningful judgments about the mission. Using these criteria we find that the mission was more successful than most missionaries thought in advancing social change, but significantly less successful in gaining ideological adherents.

It is equally important to evaluate the Indians' performance in this contest of cultures. How well did tribal peoples succeed in maintaining their cultural stability and independence? Conversely, how well did they succeed in adapting Christianity for their own purposes? In general, Indians accepted only as much "civilized Christianity" as they deemed necessary in their current situations. As long as they still possessed political autonomy, they successfully criticized or ignored the mission and deflected its revolutionary thrusts in a determined effort to preserve their Indian identity. When autonomy was lost, many Indians began to view Christianity as a powerful and effective new answer — however distasteful and upsetting — to the urgent problems that faced them. Though often incurring the wrath of their unyielding brothers, they found that Christianity could arm them with the strength to turn a social defeat into a cultural victory.

Indians — converts and resisters alike — possessed
more cultural resources and stronger instincts and
capacities for survival than historians have tended to
allow. They proved as durable in the fray as the most
zealous missionaries.

ALPHABETICAL LIST AND INDEX

*Denotes items suitable for secondary school students

Item
no.

[1]   Alden, Timothy. *An Account of Sundry Missions performed among the Senecas and Munsees; in a series of letters.* New York: J. Seymour, 1827.

[2]   Apes, William. *A Son of the Forest. The Experience of William Apes, a native of the Forest.* New York: The author, 1829.   (42)

[3]   ———. *The Experiences of Five Christian Indians of the Pequod Tribe* [cover title: . . . *or, The Indian's looking-glass for the White man*]. Boston: J. B. Dow, 1833.   (42)

[4]   Axtell, James. "The European Failure to Convert the Indians: An Autopsy," *Papers of the Sixth Algonquian Conference 1974,* ed. William Cowan. National Museum of Man, Mercury Series, *Canadian Ethnology Service* Paper No. 23 (Ottawa, 1975), 274–290.

[5]   Bagley, Clarence B., ed. *Early Catholic Missions in Old Oregon.* 2 vols. Seattle: Lowman and Hanford Co., 1932.   (17)

[6]   Barclay, Wade C. *History of Methodist Missions. Part One. Early American Methodism, 1769–1844.* 2 vols. New York: Board of Missions and Church Extension of the Methodist Church, 1949–50.   (19)

[7]   _____. *History of Methodist Missions. Part Two. The Methodist Church, 1845–1939.* New York: Board of Missions and Church Extension of the Methodist Church, 1957.

[8]   Barker, George C. "Some Functions of Catholic Processions in Pueblo and Yaqui Culture Change," *American Anthropologist* 60 (1958), 449–455.   (8)

[9]   Bartlett, Samuel Colcord. *Sketches of the Missions of the American Board* [of Commissioners for Foreign Missions]. Boston: The Board, 1872.   (25)

[10]   Bass, Dorothy C. "Gideon Blackburn's Mission to the Cherokees: Christianization and Civilization," *Journal of Presbyterian History,* 52 (Fall, 1974), 203–226.   (25, 38)

[11]   Beatty, Charles. *The Journal of a Two Months Tour; with a view of promoting religion among the frontier inhabitants of Pennsylvania, and of introducing Christi-*

anity among the Indians to the westward of the Alegh-geny Mountains ... London: W. Davenhill, 1768. (Reprinted St. Clair Shores, Mich.: Scholarly Press, 1973.)

[12] Beauchamp, Rev. William M., ed. *Moravian Journals Relating to Central New York, 1745–66.* Onondaga Historical Association. Syracuse, N. Y.: The Dehler Press.   (22)

[13] * Beaver, R. Pierce. *Church, State, and the American Indian: Two and a Half Centuries of Partnership in Missions between Protestant Churches and Government.* St. Louis: Concordia Publishing House, 1966.   (4)

[14] _____. "Methods in American Missions to the Indians in the Seventeenth and Eighteenth Centuries: Calvinist Models for Protestant Foreign Missions," *Journal of Presbyterian History* 47 (June, 1969), 124–148.

[15] Belknap, Jeremy, and Jedidiah Morse. "The Report of a Committee of the Board of Correspondents of the Scots Society for Propagating Christian Knowledge, Who Visited the Oneida and Mohekunuh Indians in 1796." *Col-*

lections of the Massachusetts Historical Society, 1st. ser., 5 (1798), 12–32.

[16]*   Berkhofer, Robert F., Jr. *Salvation and the Savage: An Analysis of Protestant Missions and American Indian Response, 1787–1862.* Lexington: University of Kentucky Press, 1965. (Reprinted New York: Atheneum, 1972.)   (5, 30)

[17]*   Blodgett, Harold. *Samson Occom. Dartmouth College Manuscript Series* 3. Hanover, N. H.: Dartmouth College Publications, 1935.   (42)

[18]   Bolton, Herbert E. "The Mission as a Frontier Institution in the Spanish-American Colonies," *American Historical Review* 23 (1917), 42–61.

[19]*   ———. *Rim of Christendom: A Biography of Eusebio Francisco Kino, Pacific Coast Pioneer.* New York: The Macmillan Co., 1936.   (15)

[20]   Bowden, Henry Warner. "Spanish Missions, Cultural Conflict and the Pueblo Revolt of 1680," *Church History* 44 (1975), 217–228.   (5, 47)

[21]   Boyd, Mark, Hale G. Smith and John W. Griffin. *Here They Once Stood: The Tragic End of the Apalachee Missions.* Gainesville: University of Florida Press, 1951.   (14)

[22] Brainerd, David. *Memoirs of the Rev. David Brainerd*, ed. Sereno Edwards Dwight. New Haven: S. Converse, 1822. (Reprinted St. Clair Shores, Mich.: Scholarly Press, 1970.)

[23] Brainerd, Thomas. *The Life of John Brainerd, the brother of David Brainerd, and his Successor as Missionary to the Indians of New Jersey*. Philadelphia: Presbyterian Publication Committee. New York: A. D. F. Randolph, 1865.

[24] [Bray, Thomas] *Missionalia: or, a Collection of Missionary Pieces relating to the Conversion of the Heathen; both the African Negroes and American Indians*. London: W. Roberts, 1727. (10)

[25] Brown, Thomas D. *Journal of the Southern Indian Mission: Diary of Thomas D. Brown*, ed. Juanita Brooks. *Western Text Society* 4. Logan: Utah State University Press, 1972. (23)

[26] Burns, Robert Ignatius, S. J. *The Jesuits and the Indian Wars of the Northwest*. New Haven: Yale University Press, 1966. (17)

[27] Caldwell, Martha B., ed. *Annals of Shawnee Methodist Mission and Indian Manual Labor School*. Topeka: Kansas State Historical Society, 1939. (38)

[28]   Caswell, Mrs. Harriet S. *Our Life among the Iroquois Indians*. Boston and Chicago: Congregational Sunday-School and Publishing Society, 1892.

[29]   Coates, Lawrence G. "Mormons and Social Change among the Shoshoni, 1853–1900," *Idaho Yesterdays* 15:4 (Winter 1972), 2–11.   (24)

[30]   Coleman, Michael C. "Christianizing and Americanizing the Nez Perce: Sue L. McBeth and her Attitudes to the Indians," *Journal of Presbyterian History* 53 (1975), 339–361.

[31]   Conkling, Robert. "Legitimacy and Conversion in Social Change: The Case of French Missionaries and the Northeastern Algonkian," *Ethnohistory* 21 (1974), 1–24.   (8, 45)

[32]   Cook, Sherburne F. *The Conflict between the California Indian and White Civilization*. Berkeley and Los Angeles: University of California Press, 1976. (Originally published in *Ibero-Americana*, 17–18, 21–24 [1940–43].)   (5, 16)

[33]   Copway, George. *The Life, History, and Travels of Kah-ge-ga-gah-bowh, (George Copway), a Young Indian Chief of the Ojebwa Nation, a Convert to the Christian*

Faith, and a Missionary to His People for Twelve Years . . . Albany, N. Y.: Weed and Parsons, 1847. (20, 42)

[34] Corwin, Charles E. "Efforts of the Dutch-American Colonial Pastors for the Conversion of the Indians," *Journal of the Presbyterian Historical Society* 12 (1925), 225–246.

[35] Delanglez, Jean, S. J. *The French Jesuits in Lower Louisiana (1700–1763). Catholic University of America Studies in American Church History* 21. Washington, D. C., 1935. (41)

[36] De Smet, Pierre-Jean, S. J. *Life, Letters, and Travels of Father Pierre-Jean de Smet, S. J., 1801–1873* . . . , ed. Hiram Martin Chittenden and Alfred Talbot Richardson. 4 vols. New York: F. P. Harper, 1905. (17)

[37] Dolfin, John. *Bringing the Gospel in Hogan and Pueblo*. Grand Rapids, Mich.: Van Noord Book and Publishing Company, 1921. (6, 38)

[38] Dominguez, Francisco Atanasio. *The Missions of New Mexico, 1776: A Description, with Other Contemporary Documents*, translated by Eleanor B. Adams and Angelico Chavez. Albuquerque: University of New Mexico Press, 1956.

[39]   Donnelly, William P., S. J. "Nineteenth
        Century Jesuit Reductions in the
        United States," *Mid-America* 17, new
        series 6 (April 1935), 69–83.

[40]   Donohue, John Augustine, S. J. *After
        Kino: Jesuit Missions in Northwestern New
        Spain, 1711–1767*. Rome: Jesuit Histor-
        ical Institute; St. Louis, Mo.: St. Louis
        University, 1969.   (16, 34)

[41]   Donohue, Thomas. *The Iroquois and the
        Jesuits: The Story of the Labors of Catholic
        Missionaries among these Indians*. Buffalo,
        N. Y.: Buffalo Catholic Publication Co.,
        1895.   (14)

[42]   Dougherty, Peter. "Diaries of Peter
        Dougherty," ed. Charles A. Anderson,
        *Journal of the Presbyterian Historical Soci-
        ety* 30 (1952), 95–114, 175–192, 236–
        253.

[43]   Dozier, Edward P. "Spanish-Catholic
        Influences on Rio Grande Pueblo Reli-
        gion," *American Anthropologist* 60 (1958),
        441–448.   (45)

[44]   Drury, Clifford Merrill. *Henry Harmon
        Spalding: Pioneer of Old Oregon*. Cald-
        well, Idaho: Caxton Printers, 1936.   (27)

[45]   _____. *The Diaries and Letters of Henry
        H. Spalding and Asa Bowen Smith relating*

to the Nez Perce Mission, 1838–1842. Glendale, Calif.: Arthur H. Clark Co., 1958. (27)

[46] _____. *Marcus and Narcissa Whitman and the Opening of Old Oregon.* 2 vols. Glendale, Calif.: Arthur H. Clark Co., 1973. (26)

[47] * Dunne, Peter Masten. *Pioneer Black Robes on the West Coast.* Berkeley and Los Angeles: University of California Press, 1940. (5, 16)

[48] * _____. *Black Robes in Lower California.* Berkeley and Los Angeles: University of California Press, 1952. (16)

[49] Eliot, John. *The Day-Breaking, If Not the Sun-Rising of the Gospel with the Indians in New-England.* London, 1647. (Reprinted in *Collections of the Massachusetts Historical Society*, 3d ser., 4 (1834), 1–23.) (6, 42)

[50] _____. *A Late and Further Manifestation of the Progress of the Gospel Amongst the Indians in New-England.* London, 1655. (Reprinted in *Collections of the Massachusetts Historical Society*, 3rd ser., 4 (1834), 261–87.) (6, 40)

[51] Eliot, John, and Thomas Mayhew. *Tears of Repentance.* London, 1653. (Re-

printed in *Collections of the Massachusetts Historical Society*, 3rd ser., 4 (1834), 197–260.)   (40, 42)

[52]   Elliott, Charles. *Indian Missionary Reminiscences, principally of the Wyandot Nation.* New York: Carlton & Porter, 1835. (Reprinted New York: T. Mason and J. Lane, 1837; Lane & Tippett, 1845; Lane & Scott, 1850.)   (19)

[53]   Engelhardt, Zephyrin. *The Franciscans in Arizona.* Harbor Springs, Mich.: Holy Childhood Indian School, 1899.

[54]   _____. *The Missions and Missionaries of California.* 4 vols. San Francisco: The James H. Barry Co., 1908–1915.   (16, 35)

[55]   Ezell, Paul H. *The Hispanic Acculturation of the Gila River Pimas. American Anthropological Association Memoir* 90.   (45)

[56]   Faust, Harold S. "The Growth of Presbyterian Missions to the American Indians during the National Period," *Journal of the Presbyterian Historical Society* 22 (1944), 82–123, 137–171.

[57]   Fenton, William N. "Toward the Gradual Civilization of the Indian Natives: The Missionary and Linguistic Work of Asher Wright (1803–1875) among the Senecas of Western New York," *Proceed-*

ings of the American Philosophical Society, 100 (1956), 567–581.

[58]   Ferry, William Montague. *Notices of Chippeway Converts American Board of Commissioners for Foreign Missions Missionary Paper* 7, 3rd ed. Boston: Crocker and Brewster, 1833.   (26, 42)

[59]   Ferry, William Montague, and Amanda White. "Frontier Mackinac Island, 1823–1834: Letters of William Montague and Amanda White Ferry," ed. Charles A. Anderson, *Journal of the Presbyterian Historical Society* 25 (1947), 192–222, 26 (1948), 101–127, 182–191.   (26)

[60]   Finley, James Bradley. *History of the Wyandot Mission, at Upper Sandusky, Ohio, under the Direction of the Methodist Episcopal Church*. Cincinnati: J. F. Wright and L. Swormstedt for the Methodist Episcopal Church, 1840.   (19)

[61]   _____. *Life among the Indians; or, Personal Reminiscences and Historical Incidents illustrative of Indian Life and Character*, ed. Rev. D. W. Clark. Cincinnati: Methodist Book Concern, 1857.

[62]   Forbis, Richard. "The Flathead Apostasy: An Interpretation." *Montana Magazine of History* 1 (Oct. 1951), 35-40.   (18)

[63]   Freeman, John F. "The Indian Convert:
Theme and Variation," *Ethnohistory* 12
(1965), 113–128.   (43)

[64]   [Friends, Society of]. *Some Account of the
Conduct of the Religious Society of Friends
towards the Indian Tribes in the Settlement of
the Colonies of East and West Jersey and
Pennsylvania . . .* London: E. Marsh,
1844.   (28)

[65]*   Gachet, Anthony Maria. "Five Years in
America *(Cinq Ans en Amerique)*: Journal
of a Missionary among the Redskins—
Journal, 1859," trans. Joseph Schafer,
Wisconsin Magazine of History, 18 (1934–
35), 66–76, 191–204, 345–359.   (15)

[66]   Gannon, Michael V. *The Cross in the Sand:
The Early Catholic Church in Florida,
1513–1870*. Gainesville: University of
Florida Press, [1965]

[67]   Garraghan, Gilbert J., S.J. *The Jesuits of
the Middle United States*. 3 vols. New York:
America Press, 1938.   (14)

[68]   Gates, Charles M. "The Lac Qui Parle
Indian Mission," *Minnesota History* 16
(1935), 133–151.   (26)

[69]   Geary, Gerald Joseph. *The Secularization
of the California Missions (1810–1846).
Catholic University of America Studies in*

American Church History 17. Washington, D.C., 1934.

[70] Geiger, Maynard, J. *The Life and Times of Fray Junipero Serra, O.F.M. Academy of American Franciscan History Publications Monograph Series* 5 and 6. Washington, D.C., 1959.

[71] ———. *Mission Santa Barbara, 1782– 1965*. Santa Barbara: Franciscan Fathers of California, 1965.

[72] ———.*Franciscan Missionaries in Hispanic California, 1769–1848: A Biographical Dictionary*. San Marino, Calif.: The Huntington Library, 1969.   (16)

[73] Gerlach, Dominic B. "St. Joseph's Indian Normal School, 1888–1896," *Indiana Magazine of History*, 69 (1973), 1–42.   (38)

[74] Gipson, Lawrence Henry, ed. *The Moravian Indian Mission on White River: Diaries and Letters, May 5, 1799, to November 12, 1806. Indiana Historical Collections* 23. Indianapolis: Indiana Historical Bureau, 1938.   (22, 34)

[75] Godwin, Morgan. *The Negro's & Indians Advocate, suing for their admission into the church* . . . London: J.D., 1680.   (9)

[76] Goodwin, Gerald J. "Christianity, Civili-

zation and the Savage: The Anglican Mission to the American Indian," *Historical Magazine of the Protestant Episcopal Church* 42 (1973), 93–110.   (11)

[77] * Gookin, Daniel. "Historical Collections of the Indians in New England," [mss. dtd. 1694] *Collections of the Massachusetts Historical Society*, 1st ser., 1 (1792), 141–226. (Reprinted New York: Arno Press, 1970.)   (34)

[78]   ———. "An Historical Account of the Doings and Sufferings of the Christian Indians in New England, in the Years 1675, 1676, 1677," *Transactions and Collections of the American Antiquarian Society* [*Archaeologia Americana*] 2 (1836), 423–534.   (34)

[79]   Graham, Hugh. "Catholic Missionary Schools among the Indians of Minnesota," *Mid-America* 13 new series 2, (1931), 199–206.   (39)

[80] * Gray, Elma E. and Leslie Robb. *Wilderness Christians: The Moravian Mission to the Delaware Indians*. Ithaca, N.Y.: Cornell University Press, 1956.   (21)

[81]   Halkett, John. *Historical Notes Respecting the Indians of North America: with Remarks on the Attempts Made to Convert and Civilize*

Them. London: Printed for A. Constable and Co., Edinburgh, 1825.

[82] Hamilton, Kenneth G. "Cultural Contributions of Moravian Missions among the Indians," *Pennsylvania History* 18 (1951), 1–15. (22)

[83] Hare, Lloyd C. M. *Thomas Mayhew, Patriarch to the Indians (1593–1682)*. New York: D. Appleton and Co., 1932. (40)

[84]* Harrod, Howard L. *Mission Among the Blackfeet*. Norman: University of Oklahoma Press, 1971. (7, 39)

[85] Harwood, Thomas. *History of New Mexico Spanish and English Missions of the Methodist Episcopal Church from 1850 to 1910*. 2 vols. Albuquerque: El Abogado Press, 1908–10. (6, 19)

[86] Hawkins, Ernest. *Historical Notices of the Missions of the Church of England in the North American Colonies, previous to the independence of the United States: chiefly from the MS. Documents of the Society for the Propagation of the Gospel in Foreign Parts*. London: B. Fellowes, 1845.

[87] Hawley, Florence. "The Role of Pueblo Social Organization in the Dissemination of Catholicism," *American Anthropologist* 48 (1946), 407–415. (8)

[88]   Heckewelder, John. *A Narrative of the Mission of the United Brethren among the Delaware and Mohegan Indians, from its commencement, in the year 1740, to the close of the year 1808.* Philadelphia: M'Carty & Davis, 1820. (Reprinted New York: Arno Press, 1791.)   (21)

[89] * _____. *Thirty Thousand Miles with John Heckewelder*, ed. Paul A. W. Wallace. Pittsburgh: University of Pittsburgh Press, 1958.   (21)

[90] * Heizer, Robert F. *The Indians of California: A Critical Bibliography. The Newberry Library Center for the History of the American Indian Bibliographical Series.* Bloomington: Indiana University Press, 1976.

[91]   Hickerson, Harold. "William T. Boutwell of the American Board and the Pillager Chippewa: The History of a Failure," *Ethnohistory* 12 (1965), 1–29.   (26)

[92]   Hoffman, Matthias M. "The Winnebago Mission: *A Cause Celebre*," *Mid-America* 13, new series 2 (1930): 26–52.

[93]   Hopkins, Samuel. *Historical Memoirs, Relating to the Housatunnuk Indians . . . under the Ministry of the late Reverend Mr. John Sergeant.* Boston: S. Kneeland, 1753. (Reprinted New York: Johnson Reprint Corp., 1972.)

[94] * Horgan, Paul. *Lamy of Santa Fe: His Life and Times*. New York: Farrar, Straus and Giroux, 1975.   (9)

[95] Hunnewell, James F. *The Society for Propagating the Gospel among the Indians and Others in North America, 1787–1887*. Boston, 1887.

[96] Hunter, Charles E. "The Delaware Nativist Revival of the Mid-Eighteenth Century," *Ethnohistory* 18 (1971), 39–49.

[97] Jackson, Halliday. *Civilization of the Indian Natives . : .* Philadelphia: M. T. C. Gould; New York: I. T. Hopper, 1830.   (29)

[98] Jennings, Francis. "Goals and Functions of Puritan Missions to the Indians," *Ethnohistory* 18 (1971), 197–212.   (7, 32)

[99] Jennings, Warren A. "The First Mormon Mission to the Indians," *Kansas Historical Quarterly* 37 (1971), 288–299.   (23)

[100] Jessett, Thomas E. "Anglicanism among the Indians of Washington Territory," *Pacific Northwest Quarterly* 42 (1951), 224–241.   (11)

[101] ———. "Anglican Indians in the Pacific Northwest before the Coming of White Missionaries," *Historical Magazine of the Protestant Episcopal Church* 45 (1976), 401–412.

[102]   Johnson, Edward Payson. "Christian Work among the North American Indians during the Eighteenth Century," *Papers of the American Society of Church History*, 2d ser., 6 (1921), 3–41.

[103]   Johnson, William. *The Papers of Sir William Johnson*, ed. James Sullivan *et al*. 14 vols. Albany: University of the State of New York, 1921–1965.   (10)

[104]   Jones, David. *A Journal of Two Visits Made to Some Nations of Indians on the West Side of the River Ohio, in the Years 1772 and 1773*. Burlington, N.J.: I. Collins, 1774. Reprinted New York: J. Sabin, 1865.

[105]   Jones, Jerome W. "The Established Virginia Church and the Conversion of Negroes and Indians, 1620–1760," *Journal of Negro History* 46 (1961), 12–23.   (10)

[106]   Jones, Peter (Kahkewaquonaby). *Life and Journals of Kah-ke-wa-quo-na-by (Rev. Peter Jones), Wesleyan Missionary*. Toronto: A. Green for the Missionary Committee, Canada Conference, 1860.

[107]   ———. *History of the Ojebway Indians; with Especial Reference to Their Conversion to Christianity*. London: A. W. Bennett, 1861. (Reprinted, Freeport, N.Y.: Books for Libraries, 1970.)

[108]   Jung, A. M. *Jesuit Missions among the American Tribes of the Rocky Mountain Indians*. Spokane, Wash., 1925.   (17)

[109]   Keiser, Albert. *Lutheran Mission Work among the American Indians*. Minneapolis: Augsburg, Publishing House, 1922.

[110] * Kellaway, William. *The New England Company. 1649–1776: Missionary Society to the American Indians*. London: Longmans, 1961. New York: Barnes & Noble, 1962.   (30)

[111]   Kelly, Henry W. "Franciscan Missions of New Mexico, 1740–1760," *New Mexico Historical Review* 15 (1940), 345–368; 16 (1941), 41–69, 148–183.

[112]   Kelsey, Rayner Wickersham. *Friends and the Indians, 1655–1917*. Philadelphia: Associated Executive Committee of Friends on Indian Affairs, 1917.   (28)

[113]   Kersey, Harry A., and Donald E. Pullease. "Bishop William Crane Gray's Mission to the Seminole Indians in Florida, 1893–1914," *Historical Magazine of the Protestant Episcopal Church* 42 (1973), 257–274.   (12)

[114]   Kessell, John L. *Mission of Sorrows: Jesuit Guevavi and the Pimas, 1691–1767*. Tucson: University of Arizona Press, 1970.   (6, 16)

[115]   ——. *Friars, Soldiers, and Reformers*: *Hispanic Arizona and the Sonora Mission Frontier, 1767–1856.* Tucson: University of Arizona Press, 1976.   (6)

[116]   Klingberg, Frank J. *Anglican Humanitarianism in Colonial New York.* The Church Historical Society Publication 11. Philadelphia, 1940.   (11)

[117]   ——, ed. *The Carolina Chronicle of Dr. Francis Le Jau, 1706–1717. University of California Publications in History* 53. Berkely and Los Angeles: University of California Press, 1956   (10)

[118]   ——. "Early Attempts at Indian Education in South Carolina, A Documentary," *South Carolina Historical Magazine* 61 (1960), 1–10.   (37)

[119]   Knox, William. *Three Tracts respecting the Conversion and Instruction of the Free Indians, and Negroe Slaves in the Colonies. Addressed to the venerable Society for Propagation of the Gospel in Foreign Parts.* [London, c. 1770]   (10)

[120]*   La Flesche, Francis. *The Middle Five: Indian Schoolboys of the Omaha Tribe.* Boston: Small, Maynard and Company, 1900; (Reprinted Madison: University of Wisconsin Press, 1963.)   (39)

[121] Lanning, John Tate. *The Spanish Missions of Georgia*. Chapel Hill: University of North Carolina Press, 1935.   (14)

[122] Leger, Sister Mary Celeste. *The Catholic Indian Missions in Maine (1611–1820). Catholic University of America Studies in American Church History* 8. Washington, D. C., 1929   (15)

[123] Lewitt, Robert T. "Indian Missions and Antislavery Sentiments: A Conflict of Evangelical and Humanitarian Ideals," *Mississippi Valley Historical Review* 50 (1963), 39–55.   (28)

[124] Loewenberg, Robert J. *Equality on the Oregon Frontier: Jason Lee and the Methodist Mission, 1834–43*. Seattle: University of Washington Press, 1976.   (20)

[125] Loskiel, George Henry. *History of the Mission of the United Brethren among the Indians in North America* . . . Trans. Christian Ignatius LaTrobe. London: The Brethren's Society for the furtherance of the Gospel, 1794. (Reprinted London: T. Allman, 1838; St. Clair Shores, Mich.: Scholarly Press, 1970.   (22)

[126] Lothrop, Samuel Kirkland. "Life of Samuel Kirkland, Missionary to the Indians," in Jared Sparks, ed., *Library of*

American Biography, 2nd ser., 15:137–308. Boston: Charles C. Little & James Brown, 1848.

[127] Love, William A. "The Mayhew Mission to the Choctaws," *Mississippi Historical Society Publications* 11 (1910), 363–402.

[128] * Lydekker, John Wolfe. *The Faithful Mohawks*. New York: The Macmillan Co., 1938.   (10)

[129] * McCallum, James Dow, ed. *The Letters of Eleazar Wheelock's Indians. Dartmouth College Manuscript Series* 1. Hanover, N.H., 1932.   (37, 39)

[130] * _____. *Eleazar Wheelock, Founder of Dartmouth College*. Dartmouth College Manuscript Series 4. Hanover, N.H., 1939.   (37)

[131] McClure, David. *Diary of David McClure, Doctor of Divinity, 1748–1820*, ed. Franklin B. Dexter. New York: The Knickerbocker Press, 1899.

[132] McCoy, Isaac. *History of Baptist Indian Missions* . . . Washington, D.C.: W. M. Morrison; New York: H. and S. Raynor, 1840. (Reprinted, New York: Johnson Reprint Corp., 1970.)   (13)

[133] McHugh, Thomas F. "The Moravian

Mission to the American Indians: Early American Peace Corps," *Pennsylvania History* 33 (1966), 412–431. (22)

[134] McLoughlin, William G. "Indian Slaveholders and Presbyterian Missionaries, 1837–1861," *Church History* 42 (1973), 535–551. (28)

[135] _____. "Cherokee Anti-Mission Sentiment, 1824–1828," *Ethnohistory* 21 (1974), 361–370. (44)

[136] _____. "The Choctaw Slave Burning: A Crisis in Mission Work among the Indians," *Journal of the West* 13 (1974), 113–127. (28)

[137] Marksman, Peter. *Life of Reverend Peter Marksman, an Ojibwa Missionary; Illustrating the Triumphs of the Gospel Among the Ojibwa Indians* . . . Cincinnati: Western Book Concern, 1901.

[138] Mayhew, Experience. *Indian Converts: or, Some Account of the Lives and Dying Speeches of a Considerable Number of the Christianized Indians of Martha's Vineyard, in New England* . . . London: for S. Gerrish . . . in Boston, 1727. (40, 42)

[139] Mengarini, Gregory, S. J. *Recollections of the Flathead Mission*, ed. Gloria Lothrop.

Glendale, Calif.: Arthur H. Clark Co.,
1977.   (18)

[140]   Mochon, Marion J. "Stockbridge-
Munsee Cultural Adaptations: 'Assimi-
lated Indians'," *Proceedings of the American Philosophical Society*, 112 (1968),
182–219.

[141]   Moffitt, James W. "Early Baptist Missionary Work among the Cherokee," *The
East Tennessee Historical Society's Publications* 12 (1940), 16–27.   (12, 38)

[142]   [Mudge, Zechariah Atwell]. *Sketches of
Mission Life among the Indians of Oregon*.
New York: Carlton & Phillips, 1854.

[143]   Mulvey, Sister Mary Doris. *French Catholic Missionaries in the Present United States
(1604–1791). Catholic University of America Studies in American Church History* 23.
Washington, D.C., 1936.   (15)

[144]   Norton, Sister Mary Aquinas. *Catholic
Missionary Activities in the Northwest,
1818–1864*. Washington, D.C.: The
Catholic University of America, 1930.   (17)

[145]   O'Daniel, Victor F. *Dominicans in Early
Florida. U.S. Catholic Historical Society
Monograph Series* 12. New York, 1930.

[146]   O'Rourke, Thomas Patrick. *The Francis-*

can Missions in Texas (1690–1793). *Catholic University of America Studies in American Church History* 5. Washington, D.C., 1927.

[147] Palm, Sister Mary Borgias. *The Jesuit Missions of the Illinois Country, 1673–1763*. Cleveland, 1933.

[148] Peacock, Mary Thomas. "Methodist Mission Work among the Cherokee Indians before the Removal," *Methodist History*, 3 (1965), 20–39.   (19)

[149] Peterson, Charles S. "The Hopis and the Mormons, 1858–1873," *Utah Historical Quarterly* 39 (1971), 179–194.   (24)

[150] Petit, Benjamin Marie. *The Trail of Death; Letters of Benjamin Marie Petit*, ed. Irving McKee, *Indiana Historical Society Publications* 14. Indianapolis: The Bobbs-Merrill Company, 1941.

[151] Phelps, Dawson A. "The Choctaw Mission: An Experiment in Civilization," *Journal of Mississippi History* 14 (1952), 35–62.   (31)

[152] Phillips, Clifton J. *Protestant America and the Pagan World: The First Half Century of the American Board of Commissioners for Foreign Missions, 1810–1860*. Cambridge, Mass.: Harvard University Press, 1969.   (27)

[153]   Phillips, George Harwood. "Indians and the Breakdown of the Spanish Mission System in California," *Ethnohistory* 21 (1974), 291–302.   (5, 17)

[154]* Point, Nicolas, S.J. *Wilderness Kingdom: Indian Life in the Rocky Mountains: 1840–1847, The Journals and Paintings of Nicolas Point*. Translated by Joseph P. Donnelly, S.J. New York: Holt, Rinehart, and Winston, 1967.

[155]   Polzer, Charles W., ed. *Rules and Precepts of the Jesuit Missions of Northwestern New Spain*. Tucson: University of Arizona Press, 1976.   (15)

[156]* Prucha, Francis Paul. *American Indian Policy in Crisis: Christian Reformers and the Indians, 1865–1900*. Norman: University of Oklahoma Press, 1976.   (4, 18)

[157]   Rahill, Peter J. *The Catholic Indian Missions and Grant's Peace Policy, 1870–1884*. Washington, D.C.: Catholic University of America Press, [1954].   (18)

[158]   Rapoport, Robert N. "Changing Navaho Religious Values: A Study of Christian Missions to the Rimrock Navahos," *Papers of the Peabody Museum of American Archaeology and Ethnology* 41:2 (1954). (6, 24)

[159]* Richardson, Leon Burr, ed. *An Indian Preacher in England: Being Letters and Diaries Relating to the Mission of the Reverend Samson Occom and the Reverend Nathaniel Whitaker to Collect Funds in England for the Benefit of Eleazar Wheelock's Indian Charity School, from Which Grew Dartmouth College.* Dartmouth College Manuscript Series 2. Hanover, N.H., 1933. (42)

[160] Riggs, Frances Mary. *Attitudes of Missionary Sisters toward American Indian Acculturation. Studies in Sociology* 72. Washington, D.C.: Catholic University Press, 1967. (38)

[161] Riggs, Stephen Return. *Tah-koo-wah-kan; or, The Gospel among the Dakotas . . .* Boston: Congregational Sabbath-School and Publication Society, [1869]. (Reprinted Boston, [1873].) (26, 38)

[162] ———. *Mary and I; Forty Years with the Sioux.* Chicago: W. G. Holmes, 1880. (26)

[163] Rister, Carl C. *Baptist Missions among the American Indians.* Atlanta: Home Mission Board, Southern Baptist Convention, 1944. (12)

[164] Robinson, W. Stitt, Jr. "Indian Education and Missions in Colonial Virginia,"

Journal of Southern History 18 (1952), 152–168.   (10, 37)

[165]   Ronda, James P. " 'We Are Well As We Are': An Indian Critique of Seventeenth-Century Christian Missions," *William and Mary Quarterly*, 3d ser., 34 (1977), 66–82.   (5, 44)

[166]   Rubenstein, Bruce. "To Destroy a Culture: Indian Education in Michigan, 1855–1900," *Michigan History* 60 (1976), 137–160.   (39)

[167]   Salisbury, Neal. "Red Puritans: The 'Praying Indians' of Massachusetts Bay and John Eliot," *William and Mary Quarterly*, 3d ser., 31 (1974), 27–54.   (7, 33)

[168]   _____. "Prospero in New England: The Puritan Missionary as Colonist," *Papers of the Sixth Algonquian Conference, 1974*, ed. William Cowan, National Museum of Man, Mercury Series, *Canadian Ethnology Service Paper* 23 (Ottawa, 1975), 253–273.   (7)

[169]   Schaeffer, Claude. "The First Jesuit Mission to the Flathead, 1840–1850: A Study in Culture Conflicts," *Pacific Northwest Quarterly* 28 (1937), 227–250.

[170] * Schultz, George A. *An Indian Canaan*:

Isaac McCoy and the Vision of an Indian State. Norman: University of Oklahoma Press, 1972. (4, 13)

[171] Schwarze, Edmund. *History of the Moravian Missions among Southern Indian Tribes of the United States*. Bethlehem, Pa.: Times Publishing Co., 1923. (22)

[172] Shea, John Dawson Gilmary. *History of the Catholic Missions among the Indian Tribes of the United States, 1529–1854*. New York: E. Dunigan and Brother, 1857. (14)

[173] Shepard, Thomas. *The Clear Sun-shine of the Gospel Breaking Forth upon the Indians in New-England*. London: R. Cotes for J. Bellamy, 1648. Reprinted in *Collections of the Massachusetts Historical Society*, 3d ser., 4 (1834), 25–67.

[174] Smith, Timothy S. *Missionary abominations unmasked; or, A view of Carey Mission . . . under the superintendence of the Rev. Isaac McCoy*. South Bend, Ind. The Beacon Office, 1833. (Reprinted South Bend: Windle Printing Co., 1946.)

[175] Spicer, Edward H. "Social Structure and Cultural Process in Yaqui Religious Acculturation," *American Anthropologist* 60 (1958), 433–441.

[176]   _____, ed. *Perspectives in American Indian Culture Change*. Chicago: University of Chicago Press, 1961.

[177] *   _____. *Cycles of Conquest: The Impact of Spain, Mexico, and the United States on the Indians of the Southwest, 1533 – 1960*. Tucson: University of Arizona Press, 1962. (6, 15)

[178]   Strong, William E. *The Story of the American Board: An Account of the first hundred years of the American Board of Commissioners for Foreign Missions*. Boston: ABCFM; New York: Pilgrim Press, 1910.   (25)

[179]   Tanis, Norman E. "Education in John Eliot's Indian Utopias, 1646– 1675," *History of Education Quarterly* 10 (1970), 308– 323.   (37)

[180]   Thwaites, Reuben Gold, ed. *The Jesuit Relations and Allied Documents 1610 – 1791*. 73 vols. Cleveland: The Burrows Brothers Co., 1896– 1901.   (14, 33)

[181]   _____, ed. "Documents Relating to the Stockbridge Mission, 1825– 48," *Collections of the State Historical Society of Wisconsin*, 15 (1900), 39– 204.   (44)

[182]   Tracy, E. C. *Memoir of the Life of Jeremiah Evarts, Esq.* Boston: Crocker and Brewster, 1845.

[183]   Van Well, Sister Mary Stanislaus. *The Educational Aspects of the Missions in the Southwest*. Milwaukee: Marquette University Press, 1942.

(39)

[184]   Vargas Ugarte, Ruben. "The First Jesuit Mission in Florida," *United States Catholic Historical Society Historical Records and Studies* 25 (1935), 59–148.

[185]   Verwyst, Chrysostom. *Life and Labors of Rt. Rev. Frederic Baraga, first bishop of Marquette, Michigan: to which are added short sketches of the lives and labors of other Indian missionaries of the Northwest . . .* Milwaukee: M. H. Wiltzius and Co., 1900.

[186]   Vittands, Alexander T. "The Trials of Pastor Cloeter: Indian Mission to Minnesota Territory, 1856–1868," *The Old Northwest* 2 (1976): 253–280.

[187]   Vogel, Claude Lawrence. *The Capuchins in French Louisiana (1722–1766). Catholic University of America Studies in American Church History* 7. Washington, D.C., 1928.

[188]   Vogel, Virgil J. "The Missionary as Acculturation Agent: Peter Dougherty and the Indians of Grand Traverse," *Michigan History* 51 (1967), 185–201.

[189]   Voght, Martha. "Shamans and Padres: The Religion of the Southern California Mission Indians," *Pacific Historical Review* 36 (1967), 363–373.   (5, 35)

[190]   Walker, Deward E., Jr. *Conflict and Schism in Nez Perce Acculturation: A Study of Religion and Politics*. Pullman: Washington State University Press, 1968.

[191]   Walker, Robert Sparks. *Torchlights to the Cherokees: The Brainerd Mission*. New York: The Macmillan Co., 1931.

[192]*   Wallace, Anthony F. C. *The Death and Rebirth of the Seneca*. New York: Alfred A. Knopf, 1970.   (28, 46)

[193]   Warner, Michael J. "Protestant Missionary Activity among the Navajo, 1890–1912," *New Mexico Historical Review* 45 (1970), 209–232.   (12, 38)

[194]   _____. "The Fertile Ground: The Beginnings of Protestant Missionary Work with the Navajos, 1852–1890," in *The Changing Ways of Southwestern Indians: A Historic Perspective*, ed. Albert H. Schroeder, pp. 189–203. Glorieta, N.M.: Rio Grande Press, 1973.   (38)

[195]   Washburn, Cephas. *Reminiscences of the Indians*. Richmond, Va.: Presbyterian Committee of Publication, 1869.

[196] Webb, Edith (Buckland). *Indian Life at the Old Missions*. Los Angeles: W. F. Lewis, 1952.

[197] Weis, Frederick L. "The New England Company of 1649 and its Missionary Enterprises," *Publications of the Colonial Society of Massachusetts, Transactions* 38 (1947–51 [1959]), 134–218.

[198] Wheelock, Eleazar. *A plain and faithful Narrative of the Original Design, Rise, Progress, and Present State of the Indian Charity-School at Lebanon, in Connecticut*. Boston: R. and S. Draper, 1763.   (6, 37)

[199] Whipple, Henry B. *Lights and Shadows of a Long Episcopate*. New York: The Macmillan Co., 1899.   (11)

[200] _____. "Civilization and Christianization of the Ojibways in Minnesota," *Collections of the Minnesota Historical Society* 9 (1901): 129–142.   (11)

[201] Whitfield, Henry. *The Light appearing more and more towards the perfect Day . . .* London: J. Bartlet, 1651. (Reprinted, *Collections of the Massachusetts Historical Society*, 3d ser., 4 (1834):100–147.)

[202] _____. *Strength Out of Weaknesse . . .* London, 1652. Reprinted in *Collections of the Massachusetts Historical Society*, 3d ser., 4 (1834):149–196.

[203]   Williams, Samuel C. "An Account of the Presbyterian Mission to the Cherokees, 1757–1759," *Tennessee Historical Magazine*, 2d ser., 1 (1931):125–138.   (25)

[204]   Wilson, Edward Francis. *Missionary Work among the Ojebway Indians*. London: Society for Propagating Christian Knowledge; New York: E. and J. B. Young and Co., 1886.

[205]   Winslow, Edward. *The Glorious Progress of the Gospel Amongst the Indians in New England*. London: Printed for Hannah Allen in Popes-head-alley, 1649. Reprinted in *Collections of the Massachusetts Historical Society*, 3d ser., 4 (1834):69–98.

[206] * Winslow, Ola Elizabeth. *John Eliot: "Apostle to the Indians"*. Boston: Hougton Mifflin Co., 1968.   (6)

[207]   Woodruff, K. Brent. "The Episcopal Mission to the Dakotas, 1860–1898," *South Dakota Historical Collections* 17 (1934), 553–603.   (12)

[208]   Wright, Asher. "Seneca Indians by Asher Wright (1859)," ed. William N. Fenton, *Ethnohistory* 4 (1957): 302–321.

[209]   Zeisberger, David. *Diary of David Zeisberger, A Moravian Missionary among the*

Indians of Ohio, ed. and translated Eugene F. Bliss. *Ohio Historical and Philosophical Society Publications*, n.s., 2–3. (Cincinnati: R. Clarke and Co., 1885), 2 vols. (21, 34)

[210] _____. "David Zeisberger's Official Diary, Fairfield, 1791–1795." Ed. and trans. Paul Eugene Mueller, *Transactions of the Moravian Historical Society* 19, pt. 1 (1963), 3–229. (21)

[211] Zens, Sister M. Serena. "The Educational Work of the Catholic Church among the Indians of South Dakota from the Beginning to 1935," *South Dakota Historical Collections* 20 (1940), 299–356. (39)

The Newberry Library
Center for the History of the American Indian
Founding Director: D'Arcy McNickle
Director: Francis Jennings

Established in 1972 by the Newberry Library, in conjunction with the Committee on Institutional Cooperation of eleven midwestern universities, the Center makes the resources of one of America's foremost research libraries in the Humanities available to those interested in improving the quality and effectiveness of teaching American Indian history. The Newberry's collections include some 100,000 volumes on the history of the American Indian and offer specialized resources for studying historical aspects of Indian-White relations and Indian linguistics. The Center also assists Native Americans engaged in writing tribal histories and developing educational materials.

ADVISORY COMMITTEE

Chairman: Alfonso Ortiz

Robert F. Berkhofer
University of Michigan

Robert V. Dumont, Jr.
Native American Educational Services/Antioch College; Fort Peck Reservation

Raymond D. Fogelson
University of Chicago

William T. Hagan
State University of New York College, Fredonia

Robert F. Heizer
University of California Berkeley

Nancy O. Lurie
Milwaukee Public Museum

Cheryl Metoyer
University of California, Los Angeles

N. Scott Momaday
Stanford University

Father Peter J. Powell
St. Augustine Indian Center

Father Paul Prucha, S.J.
Marquette University

Faith Smith
Native American Educational Services/Antioch College; Chicago

Sol Tax
University of Chicago

Robert K. Thomas
Wayne State University

Robert M. Utley
Advisory Council on Historical Preservation; Washington, D.C.

Antoinette McNickle Vogel

Dave Warren
Institute of American Indian Arts

Wilcomb E. Washburn
Smithsonian Institution